À PROPOS

Lectures choisies: niveau 1

ROBERT ARIEW
The University of Arizona

ANNE NERENZ
Eastern Michigan University

HH Heinle & Heinle Publishers
A Division of Wadsworth, Inc.
Boston, Massachusetts 02116

Publisher: Stanley J. Galek
Editorial Director: Janet L. Dracksdorf
Project Editor: Judy Keith
Assistant Editor: Nicole Baker
Design and Production: Susan Gerould / Perspectives
Cover Artist: Suzette Barbier

Heinle & Heinle Publishers is a division of Wadsworth, Inc.

Manufactured in the United States of America.

ISBN 0-8384-2369-8

10 9 8 7 6 5 4 3 2 1

À PROPOS - TABLE DES MATIÈRES

PREFACE

To Teachers and Students

Welcome to *À propos*. In this reader, you will work with many texts, including advertisements, brochures, travel guides, statistics, poems, songs, and magazine and newspaper articles. These readings were selected from a variety of authentic francophone sources, many of which were originally written specifically for French-speaking young people between the ages of 12 and 20. Each chapter in *À propos* includes two related readings. In addition, the chapters provide instruction on word analysis, comprehension, and study skills as well as strategies for approaching and understanding a text written in French. Perhaps the most important thing you will learn as you read *À propos* is that you can understand a passage written in French without understanding every word. Before beginning the first reading selection, let's think for a moment about what, why, and how we read.

What and why we read

People read for many different reasons. Make a list of the things you read in a single day, and next to each one, the reason you read it. Follow this model:

the comics	entertainment
the sports scores	information
the Dear Abby section	...

Compare your list with those of your classmates.

- How many different types of reading material did you list?
- What different reading purposes did you mention?

As demonstrated in your lists above, there are many reasons to read; we will approach the texts in *À propos* from many of these perspectives.

How we read

It is important to note that we do not always read each text in the same way. In certain situations, we read just for main ideas while in others, we read just for one or two specific details. Think about the way in which you approach a text in English when:

- you are reading about what happened in last week's episode of your favorite television series.
- you are looking for a baseball or football score.

1. In which situations do you read just for general summaries?

This reading process is called skimming. We often skim printed material to get the gist of what a passage is about or to determine if we are interested in it enough to go back and read it in more detail. In this reader, you will begin each set of comprehension activities with a skimming question in which you will identify or write out the main idea of the passage.

2. In which situations do you read for a few specific details?

This reading process is called scanning. Scanning is especially important when you are looking for a particular fact or piece of information. In this reader, you will develop your scanning skills when looking for specific details like times, dates, or prices.

Skimming and scanning

In both our native language and in a foreign language, we read for different reasons and we read using different strategies, skimming for main ideas, scanning for particular bits of information, or combining the two into a more detailed approach to a text.

The Reading Process: On becoming an effective reader

We will use a five-step reading process to help you approach and understand each text. These five steps are listed out of order below. Read steps **a–e**, and re-number them to show the order in which you think effective readers approach a written text.

a. _____ look for and understand specific details

b. _____ scan the title(s) and headings to determine the topic(s) and general overall organization of the text

c. _____ interpret the main idea and its related facts and apply this information in projects and follow-up activities

d. _____ think about the topic and remember what you already know about it as well as any personal experiences you might have had in such a situation

e. _____ read once through quickly for the main ideas

Check your answers at the bottom of the page!

Now let's think about why each step is important! With a partner, in a small group, or with your entire class, brainstorm for a few minutes about the processes effective readers use to approach and understand a printed text.

STEP 1: Scan the title(s) and headings to determine the topic(s) and overall organization

- What purposes do titles and headings serve?
- Why are they useful?
- Why should this step come first?

STEP 2: Think about the topic and remember what you already know about it as well as any personal experiences you might have had in such a situation

- Why is it important to think ahead for just a few minutes about a topic before beginning to read a text on that topic?
- How do your personal experiences help you to understand a text?

STEP 3: Read once through quickly for the main ideas

- Why is it important to first read quickly for the main idea rather than trying to understand and remember each detail right from the beginning?

STEP 4: Read again, looking for specific details

- Why is it important to read again for a more detailed understanding?

STEP 5: Interpret the main idea and its related facts and apply this information in projects and follow-up activities

- How do follow-up activities and projects help your understanding and appreciation of the material you have read?

Hopefully, this reading process will become automatic! It's a good one — one that you can use throughout your studies of French and in your reading in English for your other classes as well!

ACKNOWLEDGMENTS

We would like to express our gratitude to Charles Heinle and Stan Galek as well as to the entire Heinle and Heinle organization for their support of the *À propos/Sans doute!* project. We would especially like to thank Janet Dracksdorf for her encouragement and patience throughout the project as well as Judy Keith, Nicole Baker, and Carl Spector. We are grateful to Denise Ariew for her careful preparation of the glossaries.

Our deep appreciation goes out to the following colleagues and their students who reviewed and/or field tested the manuscript:

Bonna Cafiso, Shikellamy H.S., Sunbury, PA
Vicki Broughton, Rancho Bernardo H.S., Escondido, CA
Kathleen Cook, Cheyenne Mountain H.S., Colorado Springs, CO
Joyce Goodhue, Cherry Creek H.S., Cherry Creek, CO
Loye Hallden, Shikellamy H.S., Sunbury, PA
Lynne Harding, Randolph H.S., Randolph, MA
Lynn Heyman-Hogue, San Dieguito H.S., Encinitas, CA
Andi Laidlaw, Clague Intermediate School, Ann Arbor, MI
Judith Redenbaugh, Costa Mesa H.S., Costa Mesa, CA

And most of all, many thanks to David, Rob, and Jeff Nerenz and to Denise Ariew for their interest, understanding, and support.

Robert Ariew   *Anne Nerenz*

TEXT CREDITS

Alpo Products, Allentown, PA; **Les Nouvelles Editions de l'Arc,** Montréal; **Filles d'Aujourd'hui,** Paris; **M. Glascow Publications,** London; **Guide Michelin,** Paris, from the Michelin Red Guide France, 1991 edition and the Michelin Green Guide to New England, 4th edition, Pneu Michelin, Services de Tourisme; **McDonald's,** Paris, France; **Paris Magazine,** Paris; **Phosphore Magazine,** Paris; **Jeune et Jolie,** Paris; **Nestlé Products,** Toronto; **Les Restaurants Wendy's,** Montréal; **La Samaritaine,** Paris; **Elle, Scoop—Service de vente,** Paris

PHOTO CREDITS

Andrew Brilliant p.1, 6, 18, 19, 25, 31, 34, 37, 43, 55, 67, 73, 88, 91 right, 96, 108
Stuart Cohen/Comstock, p. 7
Mark Antman/Image Works, p. 13, 61, 79
Mike Mazzaschi/Stock, Boston, p. 49
Beryl Goldberg p. 85

C H A P I T R E 1

ALLONS AU CAFÉ!

Look carefully at the photograph; then answer the questions.
1. This café has:
   a. an interior seating area
   b. an exterior seating area
   c. both an interior and an exterior seating area
2. Look carefully at the tables.
   a. Describe their shape and overall size.
   b. What do these tables tell you about the amount of food and type of meals eaten in a café?

* Cafés are very popular spots to relax, meet and talk with friends, or simply watch the people go by. When you want to relax, to which of the following places do you go?
   — park
   — fast food restaurant
   — mall or other shopping area
   — someone's house
   — movie
   — other

Les boissons

Here are two café menus. One is from France and the other is from Canada. Before reading them, complete the following activities.

1. Make a list of:
- a. the soft drinks that you like best
- b. any other cold beverages that you might choose
- c. the hot beverages that you enjoy

2. Which beverages on your list do you think might appear on a typical French café menu? a French Canadian café menu? an American snack bar or coffee shop menu?

Read the menus and then complete the activities that follow.

AU BONNET ROUGE

CAFÉ:	AU LAIT	
	EXPRESS	0.75
THÉ:	RÉGULIER	1.50
	CHINOIS	0.75
	FRAISES SAUVAGES	1.25
	AU CITRON	1.25
	AU LAIT	0.75
TISANE:	CAMOMILLE	0.75
	MENTHE	1.25
CHOCOLAT CHAUD		1.25
JUS:	POMMES	1.25
	ORANGES	1.25
	PAMPLEMOUSSES	1.25
	ANANAS ET BANANES	1.25

Le Vendôme

café:	au lait	
	express	7F
thé:	nature	6F
	au citron	10F
chocolat chaud		10F
boissons:	Orangina	12F
	Coca-Cola	12F
	limonade	12F
	diabolo	10F
	citron	
	menthe	10F
jus:	un assortiment	10F
		14F

ACTIVITÉ 1

1. Select the statement that most appropriately reflects the content of the two café menus.
   a. French Canadian and French cafés seem to offer a larger assortment of beverages than might be available in American snack bars or coffee shops.
   b. The number and type of beverages available at a French café is very similar to what is offered in an American snack bar or coffee shop.
   c. American snack bars or coffee shops seem to offer a larger selection of beverages than French or French Canadian cafés.
2. Each café has its own special selection of beverages. Compare the cafés. Which offers more choices? How many cold beverages does each café offer? How many hot beverages?
3. For each café menu, make a list of the beverages you like, those you dislike, and those you can take or leave.
   a. Does either café offer your favorite cold beverage?
   b. Which of the hot beverages would you order on a cold day?
4. Based on the available menu items, which café would you be more likely to visit?
5. If you and a friend had $2.00 Canadian to spend, what two beverages could you order? if you had 30F?
6. What features besides beverage selection do you think are important to a young French or French Canadian person when selecting one café instead of another?

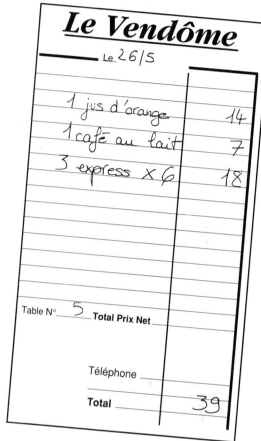

Le Vendôme

Le 26/5

1 jus d'orange	14
1 café au lait	7
3 express x 6	18

Table N° 5   **Total Prix Net**

Téléphone

Total   39

Identifying and Writing Prices

You have probably noticed that the prices are written differently on the two café menus.
1. Can you tell which café is located in which country? Match the monetary unit to the country in which it is used.
   a. francs and centimes   1. Canada
   b. dollars and cents   2. France
2. Notice that, when handwritten, numbers are formed differently. Pay careful attention to these examples:

   1   4   7   9

3. If $1.00 American is worth approximately $ .85 Canadian, can you convert these prices?
   a. café au lait, $ .75   b. jus d'orange, $1.25
4. Similarly, if $1.00 American is equivalent to approximately 6F, can you determine how much these items cost?
   a. un citron pressé, 14F   b. un Coca-Cola, 12F

Les sandwichs

Here is a menu from a French café, called *Pomme de pain*. Before reading the menu, complete these activities.

1. Make a list of your favorite light dinners and snacks. Be sure to include things that are available at home, in the grocery store, or in your favorite restaurant or eatery.

2. Here are some popular French snacks. Match each picture to its name.

a. un sandwich au fromage c. une omelette au jambon
b. une omelette au fromage d. un croque-monsieur

1. 2. 3. 4.

Read the menu, then complete the activities that follow.

LA CARTE DE POMME DE PAIN

Les sandwichs

LE PARISIEN
JAMBON FUMÉ
333 calories

LE VILLAGEOIS
VOLAILLE CRUDITÉS
360 calories

LE LYONNAIS
PÂTÉ
450 calories

LE SPÉCIAL
JAMBON/CRUDITÉS
400 calories

LE SAVOYARD
JAMBON CRU
347 calories

LE COMTÉ
FROMAGE
430 calories

LE PROVENÇAL
ŒUFS/CRUDITÉS
400 calories

Les desserts
• Le croissant • Le pain au chocolat
• Le chausson aux pommes
• La tarte aux pommes • Les glaces et les sorbets

Les boissons
• Oasis
• Eau minérale • Coca-Cola
• Café express • Chocolat chaud

ACTIVITÉ 2

1. Select the response that most appropriately reflects the content of this menu. In a French or French Canadian café, one can purchase:
   a. only beverages
   b. a variety of sweets
   c. full meals served in courses
   d. a variety of light snack foods
   e. beverages and sweets
   f. beverages, sweets, and light meals
2. Describe the sandwiches and other hot snacks.
   a. How many sandwiches are available on this menu?
   b. How many include ham?
   c. If you like ham, which of the sandwich combinations would you order?
   d. If you do not care for ham, how many alternative sandwich combinations are offered?
   e. Which sandwich has the fewest calories? the most calories?

   f. Can you purchase a croque-monsieur at this café? an omelette?
3. Most cafés offer both salty and sweet things to eat. Based on this menu, which does this café offer more of?

BONUS: The name of the café is written along the right side of the menu. Find it. It is a play on the words *pomme de pin*. Look up the meaning of this expression in a French-English dictionary.
   a. What does *pomme de pin* mean?
   b. How is this name represented graphically on the menu?
   c. Since *pain* and *pin* are pronounced the same, do you think there is a play on words in the title of the café?

Cognates

In looking over the menus in this chapter, you have no doubt recognized certain words that look like words you know in English. Words that have similar spellings and meanings in two languages are called **cognates**.

1. Give the English equivalent of these cognates found on the **Pomme de pain** menu:
   a. calories
   b. tarte
   c. chocolat
2. What other cognates can you find in this menu? List them.
3. Make a similar list of cognates from the two beverage menus provided in the first part of this chapter.

NOTES CULTURELLES

The café is very characteristic of French life—there are more than 11,000 of them in Paris. One can find at least one café on most streets in Paris. Customers can sit either inside or on the *terrasse* outside (where prices are usually a little higher). Equipped with *des jukeboxes* and *des flippers* (pinball machines), cafés are places where the French discuss the news, meet, write letters, or just relax. Cafés play an important part in French daily life.

PROJETS

1. Five of the seven sandwiches offered on the *Pomme de pain* menu are named for a city or a region in France. Find each one on a map.
2. Create your own menu. Name your café and select items from the menus in this chapter. Include on your menu a selection of beverages or cold snacks. Be sure to provide prices in Canadian dollars or in French francs.
3. Survey at least 10 of your friends during study hall, at lunch, at home, or by telephone. Explain briefly what you already know about French cafés; then get their answers to the following questions.
   a. Which beverages do you think are more popular with older people?
   b. Which are preferred by people of your own age?
   c. Can you tell why?

À L'ORAL

Select a sandwich or a hot specialty, a salad, and a dessert. Practice ordering these items with a partner. Follow this model and change roles several times:

—S'il vous plaît, Monsieur (Mademoiselle)?
—Oui. Vous désirez?
—Je voudrais... et...
—Merci.

CHAPITRE 2

ON VA À LA BRIOCHERIE!

Look carefully at the photograph, then answer the questions.
1. How many different kinds of baked goods are displayed in the window? Do they look like bakery displays in your town?
2. Which item do you think is a brioche? What is special about it?
3. Which other items can you identify? Which ones are you likely to eat for breakfast? for lunch? for a snack?

• Imagine you are at the briocherie. Write down several questions you might ask a French friend. What would you say to the waiter or waitress to order a beverage and a snack?

Les desserts

Before reading this dessert menu from the restaurant *Au bonnet rouge*, complete the following activities.

1. When you think of French cuisine, what desserts come to mind? List them.

2. Match the pastries pictured below with their names.
   a. un éclair au chocolat
   b. une brioche
   c. un croissant
   d. une tartelette aux fraises

3. Which of these four pastry names are also used in English?

4. Practice ordering a pastry with your partner. Follow the model, using the pictures below.
   —*Vous désirez?*
   —*S'il vous plaît, un éclair au chocolat.*
   or
   —*Je voudrais un éclair au chocolat, s'il vous plaît.*

   1.   2.   3.   4.

Read the menu and then complete the activities that follow.

Les desserts

Dessert du jour	2.25
Poire Belle-Hélène	1.50
Tarte maison Au sirop d'érable, au sucre ou aux pommes (toutes nos garnitures sont de fabrication maison)	1.75
Tarte aux pacanes	1.25
Fruits en coupe	2.00
Coupe glacée	3.75
Parfait à la menthe	3.95
Assiette de fromages et de fruits (Saint-Paulin, camembert, brie, cheddar, raisins, pomme)	

ACTIVITÉ 1

1. Look at the types of dessert described on the menu.
   a. Count the dessert items that include fruit. How many can you find?
   b. How many items include chocolate?
   c. How many include ice cream?
   d. How many are cakes?
2. Choose the statements that are correct. Base your answers on the desserts represented on this menu. Correct those that are false.
   a. There are many desserts made with fruits.
   b. Elaborate cakes also appear on the menu.
   c. Fruit and cheese may be selected for dessert.
   d. Chocolate desserts appear most often.
   e. Ice cream may also be ordered for dessert.
3. How many kinds of cheese are offered? How many have you tried? Which do you like?

4. Which dessert(s) would you order from this menu?
   —*Je préfère le (la, les)...*

> **BONUS:** There are several clues on this menu that indicate from which French-speaking country it came. One is found in the list of toppings available for the *tarte maison*. Use your dictionary to figure out this clue. Can you find other clues, too?

5. Interview a partner about his or her preferences; then suggest something to eat. Follow the model and change roles several times.
   —*Tu voudrais quelque chose de salé ou quelque chose de sucré?*
   —*Moi, je voudrais quelque chose de...*
   —*Bonne idée.*

Cognates and False Cognates

In the first chapter, we noticed that many words have similar spellings and meanings in French and English. These words are called cognates. Unfortunately, not all words that look alike are true cognates. Look carefully at these two examples:

1. The word *coupe* on the dessert menu—Although the word *coupe* is spelled the same in both languages, it has different meanings. In English, "coupe" refers to an automobile body style. What do you think the French word might mean?
2. The name of the café in the previous chapter: *Pomme de pain*—Although the French word *pain* looks like the word "pain" in English, the two words have very different meanings. What does the French word mean?

In order to determine whether a French word really is a cognate, think about its context. How likely is it that a dessert menu would make reference to a car? How likely is it that a café owner would use the word "pain" in the name of his establishment? Probably not a very good publicity strategy.

Always be sure to look at the whole sentence, the context, to make sure that the cognate makes sense.

Une pizza

Before reading the following advertisement for a pizza delivery service, think about these two questions.

1. What kinds of ingredients would you expect to find on a pizza?

2. Make a list of ingredients in English.

Read the advertisement and then do the activities that follow.

ACTIVITÉ 2

Reread the Spizza advertisement and answer the following questions.

1. Sizes
   a. How many sizes are there?
   b. If you and three friends wanted to order a pizza, which size would you choose?
2. Toppings
   a. Where on the menu are the toppings listed?
   b. What French word corresponds to the English word "topping"?
   c. Compare the list of toppings you made before reading the menu with the toppings offered on the menu. Which toppings do you have that are not listed?
   d. A *simple* comes with which toppings?
   e. To add more toppings to a *simple*, how much does each extra topping cost for the smallest pizza? for the medium size? for the large size?
   f. How many toppings do you get on a *suprême*, and how much do they cost for each size?
   g. Can you order a different topping on each half of a pizza?

3. Cost
   a. Une Spizza méga simple coûte *(costs)...*
   b. Une junior suprême coûte...
   c. Une super simple avec deux garnitures en plus coûte...
   d. Une méga suprême coûte...
   e. La sauce piquante coûte...
4. Service
   a. What days of the week is the Spizza open?
   b. What are its hours?
   c. Can you pay by check?
   d. Is there a delivery charge?
   e. How long does delivery take?
   f. What is the telephone number?

BONUS: The advertiser wants the customer to keep the Spizza price list handy. Where does he suggest that you keep the list?

Franglais

The *Académie française* is an official group of 40 learned people whose job is to watch over changes in the French language and to propose reforms. Despite the efforts of the *Académie française* and the French government, French people use many English words. This is called *franglais*. There are at least two examples of the use of *franglais* in the pizza advertisement. Can you find them? Hint: One is in the title of the ad; the other means "half and half."

NOTES CULTURELLES

French telephone numbers

Look at the Spizza advertisement. At the bottom is a telephone number. Does it look different from an American telephone number? How many numbers are there in an American telephone number? How are the numbers divided? You can also tell that the telephone number listed in the ad is from the Paris area because all Paris telephone numbers start with the number 4.

To make a direct call to France, you first dial the international access number, 011; then dial the country code, 33; then dial the city code (1 for Paris), and finally the telephone number of the person you are trying to reach.

Business hours

American business hours are usually 9 a.m. to 5 p.m. Some businesses, such as a pizza delivery service, might be open much longer. The Spizza delivery service is open long hours. Find their hours in the advertisement. When are they open? How are the hours given? When are they closed?

French pizza ingredients

Most of the pizza ingredients listed under *Garnitures au choix* are also commonly used in American-style pizza. Which ones are not likely to be available in your neighborhood pizzeria?

À L'ORAL

You are planning a party with several friends. You have 300 francs to spend. Decide on three Spizzas with various ingredients. Then pretend you are calling the number in France and order the Spizzas. Watch out—don't spend more than you have!

—*Allô! Spizza? Je voudrais une Spizza méga avec des champignons et des poivrons...*

PROJETS

1. Design an advertisement for a pizza delivery service or for a sandwich shop.
2. Work as a group and make one of the pizzas found on the Spizza advertisement. Use a ready-made crust and add the ingredients as they are described in the price list.

C H A P I T R E 3

TU AIMES LES FAST-FOOD?

emportez le partout..

CHICKEN SHOP

Look at the picture of the restaurant in Lyon. What kind of restaurant is it? Can you identify any words in the picture?

• What is the reputation of French cuisine? Are you surprised to learn that restaurants like this one are popular in France?

Chez Wendy

The following restaurant evaluation form is from a Wendy's restaurant. Before reading it, consider these questions.

1. If someone asked you to fill out a customer satisfaction card for a fast food restaurant, what kinds of questions would you expect to find?

2. Work with a partner and make a list of questions in English that you would expect to see on a rating form.

3. What check-off rating categories would you expect to use for the answers?

4. Where would you deposit the completed questionnaire?

Read the Wendy's evaluation form and then complete the activities that follow.

1.

Chez Wendy, nous apprécions tous les commentaires que vous pouvez nous offrir concernant nos restaurants. Veuillez remplir cette carte et la déposer dans notre boîte à commentaires ou une boîte aux lettres.

Première visite à **ce Wendy-ci:** Oui ☐   Non ☐   Aucun rappel ☐

2.

Vous êtes-vous servi de notre: Salle à manger ☐
Service intérieur pour commandes à emporter ☐
Service à l'auto ☐

3.

Pourriez-vous qualifier la:	Excellent	Bon	Médiocre	Inférieur
Courtoisie des employés	☐	☐	☐	☐
Rapidité du service	☐	☐	☐	☐
Qualité de la nourriture	☐	☐	☐	☐
Propreté du restaurant	☐	☐	☐	☐
Quelle est votre évaluation générale de ce restaurant:	☐	☐	☐	☐

4.

Avez-vous reçu exactement ce que vous avez commandé: Oui ☐   Non ☐

5.

Nom: _____

Adresse: _____

Ville/Province: _____

Restaurant situé au: _____ Code Postal: _____

Wendy's

ACTIVITÉ 1

1. The five parts of the Wendy's questionnaire are numbered 1–5. Match each part with one of these descriptions.
   a. In this section, they want to know your name and address.
   b. In this section, they want you to rate their restaurant.
   c. Here, they want to know if this is your first visit.
   d. Here, they want to know whether you use the inside seating area, the carry out, or the drive-through window.
   e. In this section, they want to know if you received what you ordered.
2. Now look at the individual sections and answer the questions.
   a. Section 1: Where does the customer deposit the completed questionnaire?
   b. Section 2: What kinds of fast food service does Wendy's offer?
   c. Section 3: What are the categories of answers? What is the best answer? the worst answer? What is the Wendy's organization interested in knowing about its employees? its service? its restaurants? its food?

BONUS: There are Wendy's restaurants in both France and Canada. From which country was this evaluation card obtained? How can you tell?

3. Before you read the evaluation form, you listed questions that you would expect to see. Which of your questions did not appear in the Wendy's questionnaire?
4. What questions appeared that were not on your list?
5. Did the Wendy's questionnaire touch on all the areas that you would have expected? If not, which one(s) didn't it treat?
6. Does it seem unusual to find American fast food restaurants in other parts of the world? What French businesses have branches in the United States?

Borrowed Words

The words *fast-food, hamburger, parking,* and *week-end* are French words that were obviously borrowed from English. There are indications that they will stay in the language and will continue to be used as French words. There are similar borrowed words in English: words of French origin that are now commonly used English words. Here are a few examples of words related to foods: *restaurant, soufflé, mayonnaise, omelet, croissant, quiche.* Look these words up in an English dictionary and find the French words from which they came. What were the original French meanings?

Try to add to your list of French words in English. Look for them in magazines, on menus, or in the newspaper. They're everywhere!

Chez McDonald

The following is a short description of the ingredients in a McDonald's salad. Before reading it, answer the following questions.

1. Salads often include several ingredients in addition to lettuce or other greens. Can you think of some other ingredients?

2. Make a list of the ingredients that you expect to find in a salad. Then check in the picture below to see if the McDonald's salads include any of those ingredients.

Read the descriptions of the McDonald's salads and then do the activities that follow.

Les salades McDonald's.

Trois variétés de salades sont proposées dans les restaurants McDonald's. Au menu : salade jardin, salade du chef et salade aux crevettes. Celles-ci sont préparées plusieurs fois par jour dans les restaurants à partir de légumes frais et d'ingrédients de tout premier choix :

salade Iceberg et Trévise, céleri, carottes, concombres, radis, tomates, œufs durs, fromage de Cheddar râpé, jambon, dinde et crevettes. Les salades McDonald's sont assorties de cinq sauces : cocktail, fines herbes, fromage bleu, vinaigrette et vinaigrette légère.

Sur simple demande auprès de l'hôtesse, vous pourrez effectuer une visite complète des cuisines de votre restaurant McDonald's. Les noms et les sigles suivants sont des marques déposées, propriétés de McDonald's Corporation : McDonald's, Big Mac, Chicken McNuggets, Filet-O-Fish.

ACTIVITÉ 2

Reread the advertisement and answer the following questions about *Les salades McDonald's.*

1. Select all the sentences that accurately describe the main idea.
  a, McDonald's offers only one kind of salad.
  b. The freshness of the ingredients is emphasized.
  c. The price of the salads is very important.
  d. The salads are made with top-quality ingredients.

2. Look on the left side of the advertisement. What three kinds of salads are described?
3. Look on the right side of the advertisement. What are the ingredients in the salads?
4. What kinds of dressings are available?

BONUS: How often are the salads made? Where are they made?

Communicating with Lists

The reading selection shows that much can be communicated with lists. In the reading, there are lists for types of salads, ingredients, and types of dressings. Consider the following example:

Les salades McDonald's contiennent des ingrédients de premier choix: salade, céleri, carottes, concombres, radis, tomates, œufs durs, fromage, jambon, dinde et crevettes.

Make lists of foods by completing the following sentences.
1. Chez McDonald on commande:
2. Les boissons chez Wendy sont:
3. À la briocherie il y a:
4. Au café on commande:

Now study your lists and find all the cognates, the false cognates, and the English words used in French. Can you find any French words that might also be used in English?

1 poulet
1 frite
1 fanta 40 cl

20 rue de la Reynie
16 bd St Michel
56 bd St Michel
6 rue du Fbg Montmartre
14 bd de Strasbourg
83 bd de Strasbourg
11 pl de Clichy
3 bd Barbes

75004 PARIS
75005 PARIS
75006 PARIS
75009 PARIS
75010 PARIS
75010 PARIS
75017 PARIS
75018 PARIS

SERVICE DE COMMANDES POUR EMPORTER DISPONIBLE

1100, rue St-Jean
Québec, Québec
694-1141

MiKES MD

MENU DE LIVRAISON

NOTES CULTURELLES

Le Fast-Food has become a new category of French restaurant most popular with young people. There are several American restaurant chains in Paris, including McDonald's (84 restaurants in France), Baskin Robbins, Wendy's, Pizza Hut, and Kentucky Fried Chicken.

PROJETS

1. Survey at least 10 of your classmates. Find out what they like to order in a fast food restaurant. What is their favorite item?

2. Using the McDonald's advertisement as a model, design an advertisement for a different food item from a fast food restaurant of your choice—for example, a super burger. Be sure to list as many ingredients as you can.

3. Bring in some ingredients and explain to the class how to make a salad of your choice.

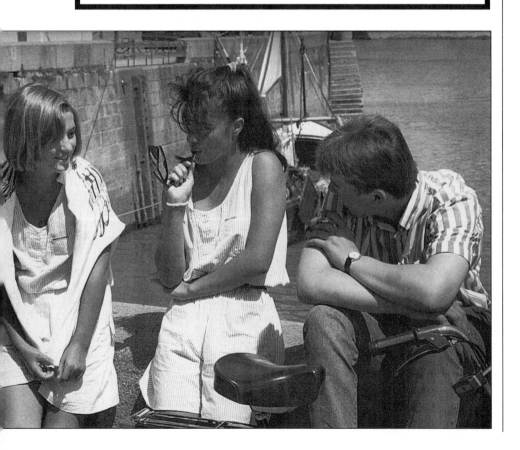

À L'ORAL

1. With a partner, imagine that you are at McDonald's and have ordered a salad. Your partner will ask you about your selection. Tell what salad you ordered and the type of dressing you chose. Then ask your partner about his or her choices.

—*Qu'est-ce que tu manges?*
—*C'est une salade aux crevettes avec une sauce fromage bleu. Et toi?*
—*C'est une salade du chef avec une sauce vinaigrette.*

2. You are walking down the street in Paris or Quebec with several friends. It is lunchtime. You all decide that you want to have something to eat.

a. First, decide what fast food restaurant or café you want to visit.

—*Je voudrais aller au café (à la briocherie, chez Wendy, chez McDonald).*
—*Moi aussi.*
(Non, allons...)
—*Très bien.*
(Alors, allons...)

b. Then order your food. Don't forget to order a sandwich or a salad, a side dish, and something to drink. Make your order as precise as you can.
—*Je voudrais...*

C H A P I T R E 4

C'EST À TOI, ÇA?

1. What is the name of the store?
2. Two items are advertised above the store's front door.
   a. Find the item names in French.
   b. How much does the item on the left cost? the one on the right?
   c. What additional information can you give about each product?

- Is there a store similar to the one in the photograph near you?
  What can you buy there?

À vendre

Here are five descriptions for electronic products from popular French magazines. Answer the questions below before reading the descriptions in detail.

1. Look at each picture; then select the correct name from the choices provided.

une calculatrice	un ordinateur	un appareil-photo
des disques	des cassettes	une radio
un téléviseur	un baladeur	une montre
un téléphone	un répondeur	

2. Ask your partner if he or she has any of the items listed above.

—*Tu as... ?*
—*Oui, j'ai...*
or
—*Non, pas moi.*

Now read the ads and do the activities that follow.

LE TÉLÉPHONE ESPION

Ce téléphone sait tout faire: il a un répondeur intégré, il peut garder jusqu'à 15 numéros en mémoire, il recompose automatiquement le numéro désiré. Panasonic KXT2422. 7 450 F. En vente chez JMD Electronics, 8, rue de Bourgogne, 75007 Paris. Tél: 45.51.68.61.

ALCATEL

TELEC 290 Téléphone sans fil, portée 150 m, protection code secret, rappel du dernier numéro, agréé P & T.

AIWA

HST 170 Baladeur récepteur, tuner. 10 stations programmables, SUPER BASS. **990F.**

CALCULATRICE SCIENTIFIQUE

FX 7000G
Programmable alphanumérique.690F
Chez Euromarché, Centre Commercial Rosny, Tél: 45.28.92.52

MONTRE FLUO

Elle va dans l'eau. Elle a la couleur des grenouilles. Elle donne l'heure et fonctionne à quartz. (280F, Hurrah chez Bathroom Graffiti, 22, rue Madeleine-Michelis, Neuilly-sur-Seine.)

ACTIVITÉ 1

1. Make a chart comparing the information supplied for the five products: *le téléphone espion, le téléphone sans fil, la calculatrice, le baladeur, la montre.* On the chart, fill in: brand name, model number, price, store name, store address, and telephone number. If the information is missing, place an X in that space.

2. Look closely at the two telephones advertised. Each has slightly different features. Compare them. Which telephone:
   a. has a fully integrated answering machine?
   b. is cordless?
   c. has an automatic redial feature?
   d. can be used up to 150 meters from its base?
   e. has a 15-number memory bank?

3. Reread the advertisements for the other three products. Which statements below are true? Correct the ones that are false.
   a. The calculator:
      is programmable.
      is solar powered.
      is especially designed for science.
   b. The walkman:
      offers a built-in tuner.
      is not programmable.
      plays compact discs.

   c. The watch:
      is waterproof.
      is green.
      is electronic.

> **BONUS:** The English word *espionnage* is related to a term used to describe one of the products. Which product? Which term? What do you think this word means in French?

4. Look at the prices of the items advertised and answer the questions.
   a. Were these items advertised in a French Canadian or a French magazine? How can you tell?
   b. Which item is the most expensive? the least expensive?
   c. Using a conversion rate of 6F to $1.00, determine how much each item would cost in American dollars. How do these prices seem to you?

5. If you could have any one of these items, which would you select? Explain your choice in French, saying:
   —*Je préfère (j'aime mieux, je voudrais) le (la)...*

Word Families

Words belong to families. One main (root) word may have dozens of members in its family. When you were reading the advertisements, you may have noticed that words seem familiar but that they have different endings or are used differently. The words seem familiar because they may have roots that you have seen before, but different endings.

For instance, consider the following English example.

The programmer programs his programmable calculator.

Notice that from the root word *program*, we have a noun, *programmer*, a verb, *to program*, and an adjective, *programmable*. There are similar word families in French. Study the following verbs in French and then find in the advertisements the corresponding nouns that are part of the same word families.

répondre (*to answer*) balader (*to walk or stroll*)

Can you also make nouns from these two verbs?

tracer (*to trace*) analyser (*to analyze*)

Le Minitel

The Minitel is a new and very special telephone service available to anyone with a telephone in France. A Minitel is a telephone that is hooked up to a small computer screen and keyboard. With a Minitel, users have access to a central information system. After connecting, one can inquire about many types of services—some free, some not. For instance, one can get directory information about any listed telephone number, shop by phone, make airplane and hotel reservations, or get information about a lot of different things, including the weather.

Which services are described in the listings below?

3615 MÉTÉO   TEMPS EN FRANCE ET DANS LE MONDE

Ce service vous donne la météo du jour et de la semaine, la carte de températures, la météo routière et la météo marine. Vous pouvez également vous informer sur le temps dans le monde: températures, pressions, humidités.

3615 FORMULE 1   HOTELS FRANCE

La "moins chère" des chaînes d'hôtels propose des chambres à 120 F. On peut réserver directement à l'hôtel de son choix (recherche par ville, région, département).

FERNAND SAIT TOUT

FERNAND vous dit tout, tout, tout sur l'éducation, en direct sur Minitel.

MINITEL 36.15 NATHAN

Before reading more about the Minitel, think about these questions.

1. What kinds of information would you like to have access to if you had a Minitel? Make a list with a partner.
2. Do you know of anything comparable in the United States?

The article at the right describes how to use another popular Minitel service, placing an order to *La Redoute*, a popular mail-order company. Read it and then do the activities that follow.

MINITEL, même le dimanche

Oui, 24 heures sur 24, 7 jours sur 7, un simple geste: 36.14 REDOUTE et votre commande est immédiatement enregistrée.

Passer commande sur Minitel: La simplicité même!

Vous allumez votre Minitel, vous décrochez votre téléphone, vous composez le 36.14, vous entrez le code REDOUTE et voilà.

- Minitel vous demande qui vous êtes: votre numéro de client, les 4 premières lettres de votre nom.
- Vous détaillez votre commande: la référence et le code de l'article, la quantité souhaitée.
- Vous choisissez votre lieu de livraison: à domicile, à une autre adresse.
- Vous indiquez votre mode de paiement: à la livraison, avec une Carte Bancaire.
- Vous confirmez votre commande.

ACTIVITÉ 2

Reread the Minitel selections; then answer the following questions.

1. What service code do you enter if you want to connect to:
   a. hotel information?
   b. weather service?
   c. a school information service?

2. Select the statements that most accurately reflect the content of the La Redoute article. This article:
   a. tells how to connect the telephone to the Minitel services
   b. gives the prices for the Minitel services
   c. explains how to place a catalog order
   d. gives a complete list of Minitel services

3. Reread the passage and provide these details.
   a. How many steps are involved in placing a Minitel catalog order?
   b. What does the system ask you first? How do you indicate who you are?
   c. What do you do next? What three pieces of information are needed for each item ordered?
   d. After placing your order, what do you do next? How many options do you have? What are they?
   e. What does Minitel ask for next? What specific choices are offered?
   f. What is the last step in placing a Minitel order to La Redoute?

Prefixes and Suffixes

Root words may be modified with **prefixes** and **suffixes** to make new members of word families. A **prefix** is a short addition to the beginning of a word, while a **suffix** is an addition to the end of the word. Prefixes and suffixes change the nature of the word—its function in the sentence and its meaning.

Make a list of some common prefixes and suffixes in English.

The Prefix dé-

The word *décrocher* is used in the article on Minitel and La Redoute: *Vous décrochez votre téléphone.* This word combines a root word *crocher* (to hook), with the prefix *dé-*. The prefix *dé-* changes the meaning of the verb. For example, the verb *faire* (to do) may be used with *dé* to make up the word *défaire* (to undo). Can you guess what the following words might mean?

1. déplacer (from *placer*, to place, to put)
2. débrancher (from *brancher*, to connect)
3. décrocher (from *crocher*, to put on a hook)

Notes culturelles

Le Minitel

The French Minitel service is becoming as common as a regular telephone. Any subscriber may request the service. Installation is free of charge. Many Minitel services—for instance, looking up a number in the directory—are free. Some services, however, do cost, and the charges appear as part of the regular telephone bill. There are over 5 million sets installed in France.

The following is a partial list of services available on the Minitel: airplane schedules and reservations, translation dictionaries, hotel reservations, road conditions and best way to get somewhere on the freeways, taxi reservations, train reservations, biographies of important people in France and around the world, banking services, job ads for young people, private mail messages to other Minitel subscribers, and want ads.

À L'ORAL

You are looking through the electronics section of a La Redoute catalog using the Minitel shopping service. Make a list in French of the items that might be offered. Using your list, discuss your current possessions with a partner. Follow the model.

—*Tu as un téléphone sans fil (un baladeur, des posters...)?*
—*Oh oui, j'ai un téléphone sans fil (un baladeur...)*
or
—*Non, mais je voudrais un téléphone sans fil...*

279ᶠ

Projets

1. Survey at least five of your classmates. Find out what possessions they have. Find out the French word for at least three of those possessions.
2. Design an advertisement for an item of your choice. Be sure to include the name of the item, the model number, the price, and the name, address, and telephone number of the store where the item may be bought.

CHAPITRE 5

Moi, J'AIME BEAUCOUP ÇA!

1. What is the name of the movie theater ?

2. What films are showing?

• Has the availability of videos made a difference in how often you go to the movies?

Au cinéma

Here is a newspaper ad for the films shown in the Rosny 2 cinemas. Before reading it, answer these questions.

1. There are many types of films—for example, adventure films like *Raiders of the Lost Ark*, documentaries like *Gandhi*, and historical reenactments like *Ben Hur*. List as many types of films as you can, and give an example of each one.

2. Working with a partner, give your opinion of each of the following types of films:

films d'aventure   films d'amour
films de science fiction   documentaires
films d'épouvante (d'horreur)   comédies

To ask for an opinion, say: **To give your opinion, say:**
—*Tu aimes les...?*   —*J'aime beaucoup les...*
                                         —*J'aime les...*
                                         —*Je n'aime pas les...*
                                         —*Je déteste les...*

Read the ad and then do the activities that follow.

ACTIVITÉ 1

1. Look over the advertisement again. Then select the statement that most closely reflects its content.

   a. This advertisement is for a single movie house.

   b. This advertisement is for a movie theater complex that shows primarily French and European films.

   c. This advertisement is for a theater where plays can be seen.

   d. This advertisement is for a movie theater complex that shows a variety of European and American films.

2. What is the name of the theater complex? How many theaters are there?

3. Does the advertisement provide:

   a. a telephone number where you might call for more information?

   b. the address or directions to the theater?

   c. the cost of tickets?

4. Beginning on what date are these films shown?

5. Based on what is stated about the parking facilities, what can you tell about this theater?

6. Review the days of the week:

lundi	vendredi
mardi	samedi
mercredi	dimanche
jeudi	

Is the theater open seven days a week?

7. There are showings of all of the films at about noon except on which two days of the week? At what times are the first showings on these two days?

8. At about what time are the latest showings for any film? On what day of the week are these late night films offered?

9. Who stars in *Allô Maman, Ici Bébé?* If you wanted to see this film on Saturday, how many showings could you choose from? To which showing would you prefer to go?

10. Who directed the film *Cyrano de Bergerac?* Who stars in it?

BONUS: Who was Cyrano de Bergerac? What can you find out about him?

11. Working with a partner, rate some of the films shown on the advertisement and others you may have seen recently. Follow the model and exchange roles.

—*Le film «Tremors» est un film sensationnel/ formidable/ intéressant/ sans intérêt.*

—*Je suis d'accord. (Je ne suis pas d'accord.)*

12. Find the cognates in the movie advertisement. Also find the English words that have been borrowed into French and the French words that have been borrowed into English.

The Prefixes mi- and demi-

When added to nouns, the prefixes *mi-* and *demi-* modify their meaning. For instance, when added to the word *nuit* (night), the prefix *mi-* changes the root to mean "midnight." When added to the noun *tasse* (a cup), the prefix *demi-* changes its meaning to "half-cup."

Guess what the following words might mean:

1. mi-temps (from *temps*, time)

2. mi-voix (from *voix*, voice)

3. demi-journée (from *journée*, day)

4. demi-frère, demi-sœur (from *frère*, brother, *sœur*, sister)

Michael J. Fox

The following character profile of Michael J. Fox has been adapted from the French teen magazine *NRJ*, an abbreviation for the word *énergie!* Think about these questions before reading this profile.

1. What magazines are popular with people of your age? with elementary school children? with older readers?

2. What kinds of information would you expect to be included in a short biography of a television and movie star like Michael J. Fox? Make a list of the kinds of information you expect to find and compare your list with several partners.

Read the article and then do the activities that follow.

MICHAEL J. FOX
Le héros de «Retour vers le futur»

C'est grâce aux films «Retour vers le futur» I et II, que Michael J. Fox a été connu en France et adopté par les kids.

Michael J. Fox est né en 1962 à Vancouver, au Canada. Il commence sa carrière à l'âge de quinze ans. Il essaye le théâtre, la radio et tourne dans un téléfilm. En 1980 il part pour Los Angeles pour devenir acteur.

Après quelques petits rôles à la télévision, Michael J. Fox devient célèbre avec la série populaire américaine «Family Ties» où il joue un adolescent. Il a un succès immédiat et il continue à jouer son rôle pendant quatre ans.

Pendant le tournage de «Family Ties» Michael est appelé par Steven Spielberg et Robert Zemeckis pour interpréter le rôle du jeune héros de «Retour vers le futur». Michael tourne le film le jour et travaille à la télévision la nuit. Ses efforts sont récompensés: «Retour vers le futur» devient un des plus grands succès de l'histoire du cinéma américain. Spielberg décide de produire deux autres épisodes du film. Son succès dans «Retour vers le futur» permet à Michael de jouer les rôles divers qu'il joue aujourd'hui.

ACTIVITÉ 2

1. Reread the passage on Michael J. Fox, then select the statement that most accurately describes the main idea of the passage.
   a. This article describes Michael's childhood in Vancouver, Canada.
   b. This article focuses on Michael's rise to television and film stardom.
   c. This article gives information on Michael's favorite foods, friends, and leisure activities.
2. Copy the chart below onto another piece of paper, and complete it based on the information you obtained from the reading.

BONUS: Take another look at this sentence from the reading passage:

Michael tourne le film le jour et travaille à la télévision la nuit.

   a. What does this sentence say?
   b. What does this imply about Michael J. Fox's character?
   c. If you were in his situation, would you have made the same decision? Be prepared to explain your choice.

Name _____

Year of birth _____

Place of birth _____

Began his career at age _____

Began his career in
— singing/recording   — television   — radio
— public speaking   — sports   — theater

First big hit
— radio   — theater   — film   — television

Role _____

Level of success _____

Length of time in this role _____

Second big hit
— radio   — theater   — film   — television

Directed by _____

Role _____

Level of success _____

Length of time in this role _____

The Prefix in- (im-)

The prefix *in- (im-)* is used to turn a word into its opposite. For instance, if the French word *succès* means "success," the word *insuccès* means "lack of success" or "no success." Guess what the following words might mean: *inégal, impoli, inévitable, indirectement.* In front of the letters *m* or *p*, the prefix *im-* is used instead of *in-.* For instance, *possible* becomes *impossible; mature* becomes *immature.*

Also note that *in- (im-)* is pronounced with either a nasal vowel or, as in English, a vowel and a consonant .
- It is pronounced with a nasal vowel when a consonant follows it: *impatient, impoli.*
- If a vowel or another *m* follows, the prefix is pronounced with a vowel and a consonant: *inévitable, inégalité, immoral.*

How would you pronounce the following: *infidèle, inégal, impossible, impoli?*

NOTES CULTURELLES

Le cinéma en France

Among the industrial nations (with the exception of the United States, which has a much larger population), France is the country with the greatest number of moviegoers. Ever since film was invented in 1895 (by the Lumière Brothers), the French have had a deep and unbroken interest in the cinema. There are many theaters in France that show many new films from around the world every year. Going to the movies is still the most popular pastime among French people today.

Le festival de Cannes

Every year an international film festival is held at Cannes. Movie producers and directors await anxiously the Cannes Film Festival to get reactions to their latest features. Prizes are awarded in several different categories of films. Many people attend the festival to get a glimpse of their favorite stars.

À L'ORAL

Select one of the following questions and interview at least five classmates. Record their answers. Combine your findings with those of other students who asked the same question, and be prepared to report your findings back to the class.

To ask for an opinion, say:
—Qu'est-ce que tu penses...

de Michael J. Fox?
du film «Retour vers le futur»?
du film «Retour vers le futur II»?
des comédies télévisées?
de «Family Ties»?

To give your opinion, say:
—J'adore...
—J'aime bien...
—J'aime...
—Je n'aime pas beaucoup...
—Je déteste...

Michael J. Fox
le film «Retour vers le futur»
le film «Retour vers le futur II»
les comédies télévisées
«Family Ties»

PROJETS

1. Match these English titles to their French equivalents.
   a. Star Wars   1. Les Dents de la mer
   b. Jaws   2. Autant en emporte le vent
   c. Gone with the Wind   3. La Guerre des étoiles
2. Make a newspaper advertisement for a movie theater complex similar to the one in this chapter. Include some of the following: the names of actors, actresses, and directors; the name of the theater complex and the number of theaters inside; its address and telephone number; the scheduled times and days of the week for all films; any special showings or exceptions to this schedule. Use additional information or graphics to make your advertisement more effective.
3. Compare a film advertisement from an American newspaper with the one in this chapter. How are they similar? How are they different?

CHAPITRE 6
VOICI MA FAMILLE!

1. How many generations are shown in the photograph? How could they be related?
2. What might they be discussing?
• What kinds of things do you talk about with your grandparents?

Les relations familiales

The following short article from the psychology section of the French magazine *NRJ* talks about how to improve relations between teenagers and parents. Before reading it, work with a partner to answer these questions.

1. What kinds of things do you talk about with your parents?

2. Should you tell them all the details of your life?

3. How would you describe your relationship with them?

Now read the article and do the activities that follow.

PSYCHO

EN PARLER OU PAS AUX PARENTS

Le conflit entre les générations n'est pas récent. Il est normal. On peut résoudre les problèmes par la confiance et la communication. Voici quelques règles.

1. Il ne faut pas mentir aux parents.

2. Rassurez vos parents; dites où vous allez, qui vous voyez.

3. S'ils vous interrogent, répondez franchement.

4. Pratiquez la diplomatie. Choisissez le bon moment quand vous demandez quelque chose.

5. Présentez votre petit(e) ami(e) à vos parents. Ils vont être heureux de faire sa connaissance.

L'essentiel est de créer un bon climat. Montrez que vous savez ce que vous faites.

ACTIVITÉ 1

Reread the article and answer the following questions.

1. The main idea of the article is:
   a. There are rules that one should follow when dealing with parents.
   b. Some things should be told to parents while others should be kept quiet.
   c. The main thing is to make them believe you are in charge.
   d. The relationship between parents and children is not an easy one.
   e. Sometimes a little white lie is the best solution.

2. Match the following statements with the appropriate numbers in the article.
   a. Be diplomatic.
   b. Never lie to your parents.
   c. Reassure them by telling them where you are going and with whom.
   d. Introduce your boy(girl)friend to them.
   e. If they ask questions, answer frankly.

3. According to the article, what is the most important rule?

4. Which rule do you think is the most important? the least?

5. Working with a partner, discuss which of the following rules you think are a good idea and agree with. Follow the model and exchange roles.
   a. Il faut mentir aux parents.
   b. Il faut répondre franchement.
   c. Il ne faut pas présenter les amis.
   d. Il faut dire où on va.

   —*Il faut mentir aux parents.*
   —*Non, je ne suis pas d'accord. C'est une mauvaise idée.*
   or
   —*Je suis d'accord. C'est une bonne idée.*

The Prefix re-

When the prefix *re-* is added to a verb, the verb's meaning changes. For example, the verb *faire* (to do) may be used with the prefix *re-* to make up the word *refaire* (to redo). Look in the article and find the prefix *re-* used with the following verb: *rassurez*. The verb *assurer* means "to assure." What does *rassurez* mean? Notice that the *re-* changes to *r-* before a vowel.

Now look at the following words. Add the prefix *re- (r-)* and try to tell what the new words might mean.
1. accrocher (to put the telephone on the hook, to hang up)
2. composer (to dial a number, to compose)
3. appeler (to call)
4. dire (to say)
5. demander (to ask)

La famille aujourd'hui

The following short article is adapted from a book about recent changes in the French family. Before reading it, think about these questions.

1. Do you and your friends generally get along with your parents?
2. With whom do you talk when you have big problems? when you have less serious ones?
3. What role does your family play in solving your problems?

Now read the article and do the activities that follow.

FAMILLE, *je vous aime*

Le conflit des générations ne pose plus de problèmes sérieux. Toutes les enquêtes montrent que les jeunes Français ne connaissent pas de grands problèmes avec leurs parents. Ils communiquent généralement bien avec eux, même si on ne parle pas de certains sujets en famille. Ils ne manquent pas d'affection, même si l'amitié des amis vient souvent en première place.

La famille est un lieu confortable. On parle plus volontiers aux parents (à la mère en particulier) qu'aux professeurs. Voici les résultats d'une enquête récente:

Comment trouvez-vous vos parents?

• Ils me comprennent	**66%**
• Ils sont dépassés	**15%**
• Je suis en conflit avec eux	**3%**
• Pas de réponse	**16%**

Qu'est-ce qu'il manque aux enfants pour être complètement heureux? En réalité peu de choses:

• La possibilité de parler de certains problèmes, concernant par exemple les relations entre garçons et filles.

• Peut-être aussi un peu plus d'argent de poche.

ACTIVITÉ 2

Reread the article and answer the following questions.

1. The main idea of the article is (choose all that apply):
   a. For the most part, the generation gap no longer exists.
   b. There are certain things that young people do not discuss with their parents.
   c. Most children are in conflict with their parents.
   d. Young people confide mostly in their professors.

2. Tell if the following statements are *vrai* or *faux*. Correct the ones that are false.
   a. On parle généralement au père.
   b. Le conflit des générations n'existe pas aujourd'hui.
   c. Les enfants communiquent avec leurs parents.
   d. La majorité des enfants trouvent leurs parents dépassés.
   e. Les enfants manquent d'argent de poche.

3. What percentage of young people think their parents:
   a. are understanding?
   b. do not understand them?
   c. are too old-fashioned to understand them?

4. According to the article, what two things do young people need to be truly happy?

Suffixes

As we saw in Chapter 4, suffixes are additions to the ends of words. Adding suffixes to the end of words changes their meanings.

The Suffixes -aire and -able

Some suffixes are added to the end of a root word to change it from one part of speech to another. The following suffixes make adjectives from verbs.

- the suffix -aire: supplémenter → supplémentaire
  séances supplémentaires
- the suffix -able: programmer → programmable
  calculatrice programmable

The Suffix -ment

The suffix -ment makes an adverb from an adjective. It is equivalent to the English suffix -ly. To make an adverb from an adjective, take the feminine form of the adjective and then add -ment to it.

complet → complète → complètement
général → générale → généralement

Make adverbs from the following adjectives: *amical, rapide, confortable*

NOTES CULTURELLES

La famille

The average number of children per couple in France is 1.8. This figure compares very closely with the statistics in the United States.

Les animaux

The French are avid pet owners. One out of two families owns a pet. There are as many dogs in France as there are children under the age of 11—approximately 10 million. Approximately one-third of French families own a dog, while one family out of five owns a cat.

PROJETS

1. Give some advice to a younger brother or sister about how to get along with parents or friends. Model your advice on the readings in this chapter.
2. Is there really a generation gap? Write an essay in English to argue for or against the idea.
3. Make a poster illustrating the most important rules to remember about getting along with parents or family members, friends, or teachers. Write your rules in French.

À L'ORAL

Working with a partner, ask about his or her family, including his or her brother (ton frère), and sister (ta sœur), aunt (ta tante) and uncle (ton oncle). Ask what their names are and where they live. Follow the model. Then switch roles.

—Tu as un oncle?
—Oui.
—Comment s'appelle ton oncle?
—Il s'appelle Robert.
—Où habite ton oncle Robert?
—Il habite à Chicago.

CHAPITRE 7

FAISONS CONNAISSANCE DE LA VILLE!

Look carefully at the photograph.

1. Which words best describe the scene?
Cette ville est: a. moderne b. ancienne c. pittoresque

2. How does this city differ from the cities in your part of the country?

3. Check the photograph for the following features:
a. width of street b. types of vehicles c. signs and lights d. building design
What do these features tell you about the city? What activities take place in this district?

4. Do you think that the people in this scene live in this city? Are they going to work? running errands? on their way to an entertainment event? Be prepared to justify your answer.

Les amusements

Here are some announcements of entertainment events. Before you read them, look over the following list of places and tell which ones are for errands (*pour faire des courses*) and which ones are for entertainment (*pour m'amuser*).

—*Je vais à (au)... pour faire des courses.*
—*Je vais à (au)... pour m'amuser.*

—la gare	—la discothèque	—la piscine
—le cinéma	—le café	—le restaurant
—le parc	—le stade	—le bureau de poste

Now read the announcements and complete the activities that follow.

LE GRAND CIRQUE DU ZINGARO

Troisième et ultime prolongation d'un chef-d'œuvre équestre et musical. À ne pas rater.

91, bd de Charonne, 11ᵉ. 43.71.26.55. Jusqu'au 17 mai à 20h 30.

ballets · danse

Bastille, 76, rue de la Roquette, 43 57 42 14. Jusqu'au 30 avril inclus à 20h : « Circumvesuviana » chorég. de Paco DECINA avec A. Battaglia, P. Decina, D. D'Urso, S. Lessard, C. Rousier, C. Diaconale, C. Le Prince.

TERENCE TRENT D'ARBY

Contrairement aux apparences, Terence Trent d'Arby ne doit pa son succès instantané à son loo mi-Marley mi-Noah. C'est un authentique créateur à la séduction indéniable. Découvert par les Parisiens au printemps dernier à la Cigale, il est de retour à Paris. **Zénith, porte de Pantin. 42.46.00.00. Le 17 mai à 20 h. Locations Fnac, Clémentine.**

ORCHESTRE D'ATLANTA

Ouverture du 4ᵉ Festival international d'Orchestres du TMP-Châtelet avec les Chœurs et l'Orchestre d'Atlanta. Leur chef, Robert Shaw, a choisi pour la circonstance la *Symphonie de psaumes* de Stravinski et la *Neuvième* de Beethoven. Bref, un copieux menu!

TMP, place du Châtelet, 1ᵉʳ. 42.33.44.44. Le 2 à 20h 30.

JOE COCKER

Retour d'un vieux routier à la voix rauque éraillée... Joe Cocker a beau n'être plus de toute première fraîcheur, avec le rock-blues puissant de son dernier album, *Unchain my heart*, il conserve toujours un contingent d'admiratrices éperdues. Pour elles, ce drôle de crooner revient au Zénith où il triomphait déjà il y a à peine deux mois ! **Zénith, porte de Pantin. 42.46.00.00. Le 22 mai à 20 h. Locations Fnac. Clémentine.**

D. Ferry

ENSEMBLE ORCHESTRAL DE PARIS

Mélodies et musique de chambre française à l'Ensemble orchestral de Paris. La soprano Rachel Yakar, la pianiste Claude Lavoix et les chefs de pupitre de cette formation se sont donnés rendez-vous pour célébrer Debussy, Ravel et Roussel.

Salle Gaveau, 45, rue La Boétie, 8ᵉ. 45.63.20.30. Le 2 à 20h 30.

FOOTBALL

8 juin, 20 h.:
« Finale de la Coupe de France de Football » au Parc des Princes Porte Saint-Cloud, XVIᵉ, et à la télévision.

Introduction to Outlining

Whenever you need to write a paragraph about any subject, the first thing to do is to make an outline that includes the information that the paragraph will contain. For instance, imagine that you were asked to write a paragraph about a concert. In the paragraph you would have to provide several pieces of information, including the nature of the event, the date and time when it will take place, the location of the event, and a brief commentary about the event. The outline of the paragraph might look like this:

I. Concert de Joe Cocker
  A. un concert de rock
  B. avec Joe Cocker en personne *(live)*
II. Lieu, date et heures
  A. au Zénith
  B. le 22 mai
  C. un concert à 20h
III. Un concert de grande qualité
  A. beaucoup d'admirateurs
  B. un rock-blues formidable

ACTIVITÉ 1

1. Reread the announcements and then indicate whether each statement is true or false. Correct the ones that are false.
  a. Announcements for both places of business and entertainment locations are included.
  b. The announcements include a variety of types of events.
  c. More sporting events are advertised than any other kind.

2. Summarize the most important information about each announcement, using the following outline:

  WHAT: Indicate the type of event *(un match de sport, un concert...)*
  WHO: State the name of the artist or group.
  WHERE: Give the address and the telephone number.
  WHEN: State the date(s) and the time of the event.
  SUMMARY: Provide just one or two important details about the event.

BONUS: Which event will be televised? Which one is a return engagement, with the original performance having taken place two months earlier?

3. Imagine that these entertainment events are available in your home town.

To invite someone to go with you, say:
—*Nous allons au match de foot / au ballet / au concert de Terence Trent d'Arby. Ça t'intéresse?*
or
—*Ça t'intéresse d'aller au concert? au ballet? au cirque? au cinéma?*

To accept an invitation, say:
—*Bien sûr! Avec plaisir!*

To refuse an invitation, say:
—*Je regrette. Ce n'est pas possible.*

Now invite several different people to several different events. Keep track of their responses.

Quelques musées français

One way to get acquainted with Paris is to visit its museums, which are located in different neighborhoods, or *quartiers,* throughout the city. Before reading the article, test your knowledge about museums by telling if each of the following sentences is *vrai* or *faux.*

1. Once the palace of the French royalty, the Louvre is now the largest art museum in the world.
2. Although the Louvre houses a wide variety of collections, the Impressionist collection (works dating from 1870 to 1915) is not displayed there.
3. The well-known bronze sculpture **The Thinker** *(Le Penseur)* was created by Auguste Rodin (1840-1917), whose works are on display at the Musée Rodin in Paris.

Now read the article on the national museums and do the activities that follow.

Answers: 1v, 2v, 3v

LES MUSÉES NATIONAUX

Les musées nationaux reçoivent chaque année des millions de visiteurs.

COMBIEN DE MUSÉES Y A-T-IL?

Il y a en France 34 musées nationaux, une trentaine de musées locaux et quelque 900 musées contrôlés par l'état. Il y a 51 musées dans la ville de Paris.

LE MUSÉE LE PLUS CÉLÈBRE

Le Louvre, ancienne résidence royale, est le plus célèbre des musées nationaux. Il y a 6 000 peintures, 2 250 sculptures, 46 000 gravures, 90 000 dessins et plus de 150 000 pièces d'antiquités égyptiennes, orientales, grecques et romaines. Visitez aussi le hall Napoléon et les fossés médiévaux. Voici une publicité pour le grand musée du Louvre.

Louvre

Palais du Louvre
75001 Paris
Tél. (1) 40 20 51 51
Métro : Palais Royal, Louvre

• Antiquités égyptiennes, orientales, grecques, étrusques et romaines. Peintures. Sculptures. Mobilier et objets d'art. Arts Graphiques.
Ouvert de 9h à 18h, les jeudi, vendredi, samedi et dimanche.
Nocturne les lundi et mercredi jusqu'à 21h45.
Fermé le Mardi

• Le hall Napoléon, les salles d'Histoire du Louvre, les fossés médiévaux l'Auditorium, la librairie et les restaurants sont ouverts tous les jours de 9h à 22h. Les expositions temporaires de 12h à 22h.

LE MUSÉE RODIN

Il existe actuellement deux musées Rodin: un musée à Paris et un autre dans la banlieue de Meudon. Ces deux musées sont réunis pour former un seul musée qui fait honneur aux œuvres du grand sculpteur Rodin. À l'hôtel Biron à Paris on trouve les bronzes, les marbres et les tableaux de la collection Rodin. À la villa des Brillants à Meudon se trouve la maison familiale et l'atelier de Rodin. Voici une publicité pour le musée à Paris.

Auguste Rodin

Hôtel Biron
77, rue de Varenne
75007 Paris
Tél. (1) 47 05 01 34
Métro : Varenne
Ouvert de 10h à 17 h du 1er octobre au 31 mars, et de 10h à 17h45 du 1er avril au 30 septembre
Fermé le Lundi
Closed on Mondays

• Œuvres et collections d'Auguste Rodin.
• *Works and collections of Auguste Rodin.*

ACTIVITÉ 2

1. Reread the passage, then select the statement that most appropriately reflects the main idea of this passage.
   a. One cannot really get to know Paris without a visit to the many museums located throughout the city.
   b. There are more museums in France than in the United States.
   c. The artistic and historic heritage of the French is preserved in its many and varied museums located in Paris and throughout the country.
2. How many national museums are there in France?
3. How many museums are there in the city of Paris alone?
4. Now scan the announcements to find the following facts and information.

   a. Are the two museums open seven days a week? If not, on what day(s) are they closed?
   b. What are the hours during which the museums are open?
   c. Are they accessible by metro?
5. Would you find the following exhibits in the Louvre, in the Musée Rodin, or in neither museum?
   a. des antiquités égyptiennes, grecques et romaines
   b. des photographies
   c. des objets de l'empereur Napoléon
   d. des œuvres et collections du sculpteur Rodin
6. Which of the exhibits described above interests you the most?

Les 34

MUSÉES

NATIONAUX

Using Titles and Headings

When you are first looking over a passage, it is important to examine the title, the main headings, and the subheadings to determine:
- the subject of the article
- how each section of the passage relates to the main idea
1. Reread the article on the museums and locate the title. Headings and subheadings are smaller titles. How many main headings are there? How many subheadings are there?
2. Quickly read over the following title and headings for what might be an article on getting acquainted with Quebec City. Organize under each section of the outline the corresponding main headings and subheadings.

Quoi faire à Québec
I. Main heading
  A. Subheading
  B. Subheading
  C. Subheading
  D. Subheading
  E. Subheading

II. Main heading
  A. Subheading
  B. Subheading
  C. Subheading
  D. Subheading
  E. Subheading

Main headings: les sports en plein air; les fêtes
Subheadings: le ski; le carnaval; la fête de la pâtisserie; le hockey; la fête de l'érable; le canotage; le cyclisme; le festival folklorique de la Baie-Saint-Paul; la fête du bleuet; la pêche

NOTES CULTURELLES

Les arrondissements

Paris is divided into 20 districts, called *arrondissements*. Each *arrondissement* corresponds to a

neighborhood and has its own postal code. For instance, the postal code 75007, which is the code for the neighborhood of the Musée Rodin, contains the number 75, which represents Paris, and the number 07, which represents the 7th *arrondissement*. Check the museum descriptions to determine in which *arrondissement* the Louvre is located.

PROJETS

1. Make a list of museums with artistic or historical collections in and around your hometown. Prepare a museum announcement for one of them, including descriptions of the various collections as well as information on the days and hours of operation, admission fees, and so on.
2. Getting to know a city is fun and important. Prepare a visitor's guide that would help newcomers get acquainted with your hometown or another important city in your state.
3. When was the last time you visited a museum? What kind of museum was it (art, natural history, historical …)? What works or exhibits did you especially like? Are there particular styles or works of art that you like? that you dislike? Be prepared to describe one of them.
4. Research a French artist. Be prepared to tell the class about him or her and the type of art he or she creates.

À L'ORAL

1. How often do you visit the museums in or near your home town? Ask and answer this question with a partner.

   —*Tu vas souvent au musée?*
   —*Je vais… au musée.*
     assez souvent
     de temps en temps
     quelques fois
     rarement

2. Knowing and being able to ask for and tell the date of entertainment events is especially important when making plans.
   a. Review the names of the months in French.

janvier	juillet
février	août
mars	septembre
avril	octobre
mai	novembre
juin	décembre

   b. Look carefully in the announcements to determine which of the following patterns is used when writing a date:
   month + day
   or day + month.
   c. Ask and state the dates for the Terence Trent D'Arby concert (*le 17 mai*), the Joe Cocker concert (*le 22 mai*), and the Ensemble Orchestral de Paris concert (*le 2 mai*).

To ask the date, say:
—*Quelle est la date du concert?*

To tell the date, say:
—*Le concert? C'est le 17 mai.*

CHAPITRE 8

OÙ SE TROUVE...?

1. Who do you think the people in the photograph might be?
   a. Which of them probably live in the city shown?
   b. Why do you think they happen to be on this street corner?
2. Look closely at the policeman's uniform. What distinctive features do you notice?
3. Imagine the conversation that is probably taking place.
   a. Which French expressions that you already know might be used in this situation?
   b. What additional expressions might you need to learn in order to communicate in a situation like this one?

Saint Jean de Luz

This photograph and map come from a tour book for Saint Jean de Luz, a little town located near Biarritz in France. First, refer to a large map of France to answer these questions.

1. Find Biarritz on a map. Is Saint Jean de Luz also marked?
2. What body of water is located near Biarritz?
3. Knowing that Saint Jean de Luz is close to Biarritz, what geographical features would you also expect to find on this city map?
4. The French word for "light" is *lumière*. The word *luz* also means "light," but it is not a French word. From what language do you believe this word was borrowed? Can you explain why?
5. City maps included in such a guide book generally show buildings of more interest to tourists than to people who actually live in the city. Scan this list and be prepared to tell which items are likely to be marked on a map and which ones probably are not indicated.

un boulevard	une église	un parking
une école	une avenue	une bibliothèque
une épicerie	la poste	un café
un lycée	une rue	l'office de tourisme
une place	une boucherie	une université
un parc	une boulangerie	un cinéma
un hôtel	une gare SNCF	une cathédrale

Now look at the map and do the activities that follow.

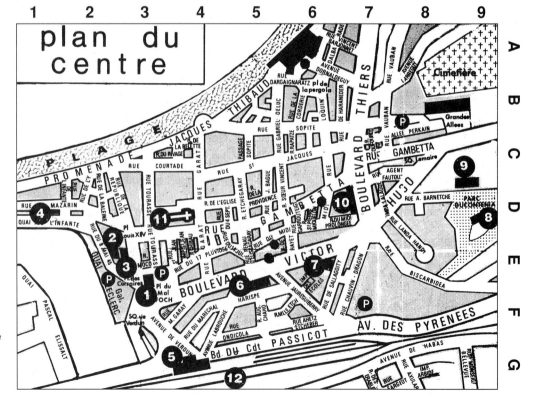

1 Office de Tourisme
2 Mairie
3 Maison de Louis XIV
4 Maison de l'Infante
5 Gare SNCF
6 Halles
7 P.T.T.
8 Théâtre de la Nature
9 Pompiers
10 Trinquet Maîtena
11 Église St-Jean-Baptiste
12 Gymnase Urdazuri
P Parkings
● Cinémas

ACTIVITÉ 1

1. This map shows which of the following?
   a. the métro and bus routes in Saint Jean de Luz
   b. the section of Saint Jean de Luz where most tourist sites are located
   c. the hotels and restaurants most tourists would like to visit

2. Survey the map to determine these general features.
   a. What are the main streets in Saint Jean de Luz? How can you tell that these are more important than the others?
   b. How many parking lots are there? movie theaters?
   c. Locate the beach. Is the part of the city shown on the map the only part that borders the water? How can you tell?
   d. Is there railroad service in Saint Jean de Luz?

3. Now examine the map more closely and tell if each statement is *vrai* or *faux*.
   a. L'Office de Tourisme se trouve à la place du Maréchal Foch.
   b. La Mairie se trouve loin de l'Office de Tourisme.
   c. La Maison de Louis XIV se trouve à côté de la Mairie.

   d. La Maison de l'Infante se trouve entre la rue Mazarin et la rue de l'Infante.
   e. La gare est loin du cimetière.
   f. La poste se trouve au coin du boulevard Victor Hugo et du boulevard Thiers.
   g. Les pompiers sont en face du parc.
   h. L'église Saint-Jean-Baptiste se trouve près du centre de la ville.

4. Imagine that you are at the train station. Follow these directions and then tell where you will be.
   a. Quittez la gare et prenez l'avenue de Verdun jusqu'à la place du Maréchal Foch. Traversez la place et continuez tout droit dans la rue Tourasse. Continuez tout droit jusqu'à la promenade Jacques Thibaud. Où êtes-vous?
   b. Quittez la gare et allez immédiatement à droite sur le boulevard du Commandant Passicot. Tournez à gauche dans la rue Chauvin Dragon. Continuez tout droit, ensuite tournez à droite sur le boulevard Victor Hugo. Prenez la troisième rue à droite jusqu'au bout. Où êtes-vous?

Reading a Map

Being able to read a map is essential when getting acquainted with a new location. Notice these important features:
- Maps often provide a grid of numbers and letters along with an index that gives the coordinates of important places. To find a particular building, you first look up its coordinates in the index. You then pinpoint its location on the map by finding the point at which a line drawn from the number and another drawn from the letter coincide. On the map of Saint Jean de Luz, what building is located at D6? at G4? at C9?
- Maps often include a scale indicating the correspondence between distance on the map and feet, yards, and miles or meters and kilometers. Is such a scale provided on the map of Saint Jean de Luz? Can you explain why?
- Certain locations on the map are represented with symbols. Which ones are they? What other location/symbol correspondences might travelers find helpful?
- Many maps indicate the cardinal directions (north, south, east, west). Why do you think this map does not? Do you think it might be helpful? Knowing what you do about the general location and geographical features of Saint Jean de Luz, which way do you think north is?

Promenade dans le vieux Montréal

The following brochure describes a walking tour in Old Montreal. Before taking the tour, think about these questions.

1. What do you already know about Canada—its location, capital, major cities, history, and way of life?

2. What do you know in particular about French-speaking Canadians?

3. Did you know that Montreal, founded in 1642 and originally named Ville-Marie, is the second largest French-speaking city in the world?

Follow along as we take a short walking tour of Old Montreal. Then do the activities that follow.

La place d'Armes

Notre point de départ est la place d'Armes. Le monument au centre est en l'honneur de Paul de Chomedey, sieur de Maisonneuve. Il a fondé Montréal en 1642.

Notre-Dame de Montréal

En face de la place d'Armes, vous voyez Notre-Dame de Montréal. C'est probablement la plus belle église en Amérique du Nord.

L'Hôtel de Ville

Continuez tout droit dans la rue Notre-Dame jusqu'à l'Hôtel de Ville, sur votre gauche. Passez à droite de l'Hôtel de Ville dans la place Vauquelin et promenez-vous derrière l'Hôtel de Ville sur le Champ-de-Mars. Retournez dans la rue Notre-Dame.

Notre-Dame-de-Bonsecours

Continuez tout droit dans la rue Notre-Dame jusqu'à la rue Bonsecours. Tournez à droite. Au bout de la rue, vous allez voir la chapelle de Notre-Dame-de-Bonsecours. On l'appelle aussi la «chapelle des Matelots». Dans l'église, on peut voir plusieurs bateaux miniatures laissés par des marins. En plus, on peut monter à un observatoire pour regarder le port.

Quittez la petite église et allez tout droit dans l'avenue Saint-Paul. Continuez tout droit jusqu'à la rue Saint-Sulpice. Tournez à droite et suivez cette rue pour retrouver la place d'Armes, notre point de départ!

ACTIVITÉ 2

1. Which statement most closely reflects the main idea of the passage?
   a. The walking tour provides a broad overview of the city of Montreal.
   b. This walking tour provides a brief introduction to some of the oldest religious and governmental sites in Montreal.
   c. This walking tour highlights the important commercial and industrial role Montreal plays due to its position on the Saint Lawrence Seaway.

2. Reread the passage; look especially for the following important details.
   a. Where are the miniature sailing ships located?
   b. Whose statue is in *la place d'Armes* and why is he remembered?
   c. According to the article which is the most beautiful church in North America?
   d. What is the area behind the *Hôtel de Ville* called?
   e. What is another name for *la chapelle des Matelots?*

> **BONUS:** In the guided tour, find at least six terms (a) that indicate where a building is located or (b) that describe directions.

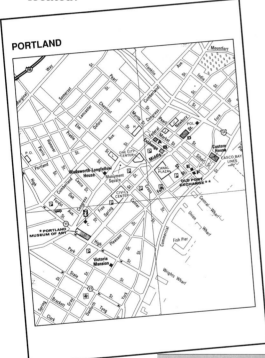

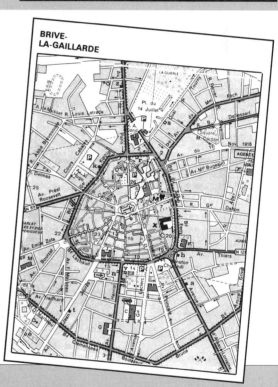

Reading a Map

American tourists sometimes find themselves quite lost even in small French cities. Perhaps you can tell why! Look carefully at the two city maps above.

1. Which city appears to be designed on a squared-off, right-angle plan, where most streets run parallel or perpendicular to each other?

2. Which city appears to be designed on a rounded-off, curved-line plan, where main streets function like spokes in a wheel with smaller streets connecting across the spokes?

3. On which plan are street names likely to change most often and house numbers likely to consist of only one or two digits?

4. Why do you think that American or even Canadian tourists might more easily become lost when visiting a French city than would French tourists in North America?

NOTES CULTURELLES

Canada covers most of the northern part of the North American continent and has an area larger than that of the United States. It is a country with over 26 million people, two-thirds of whom live near the border with the United States. Canada has 10 provinces—Alberta, British Columbia, Manitoba, New Brunswick, Newfoundland, Nova Scotia, Ontario, Prince Edward Island, Quebec, and Saskatchewan. There are French speakers in many provinces, although most of them live in Quebec.

PROJETS

1. The buildings in Old Montreal recall the most important events in the history of the city, including:
   a. the founding of the city by Maisonneuve
   b. the establishment of French missionaries in "New France"
   c. the exploits of the explorers as they traversed lakes and rivers in their quest to cross the continent
   d. the interactions between Native Americans and fur traders during the fur trade era
   e. the British colonial regime
   f. the birth of the Canadian confederation
   g. the subsequent growth and development of Montreal as the world's second largest French-speaking city

   Select one of these historical periods, or another important event in the history of French-speaking Canada, and prepare a short report to share with your classmates.

2. Do the buildings described seem old by North American standards? Are there any buildings dating to this period in your home town? Do you think that the North American concept of "an old building" is different from a European definition of what is "old"? Why might this be true? Tell your friends about the old buildings in your area.

3. Write a description of one of the oldest buildings in or near your home town.

4. Research famous Canadians such as actors Michael J. Fox or Rich Little, director Norman Jewison, or news anchor Peter Jennings. Write a report to present in class.

À L'ORAL

Working with a partner, discuss where buildings in your neighborhood are located relative to each other. Follow the model and exchange roles.

—*Où est ...*
   le café?
   le cinéma?
   le parc?
   la poste
   la bibliothèque?
—*Le café est ... la bibliothèque.*
   à côté de (next to)
   en face de (across from)
   près de (near)

CHAPITRE 9

ALLONS AU FESTIVAL!

1. What do you think the people in the photograph are doing?
2. What do you notice about what they are wearing or carrying? What function might those things serve, or what might they symbolize?
3. Where do you think this event is taking place? If you were there, would you want to participate?

Les festivals

Festivals often celebrate cultural and ethnic diversity. The following announcement describes a cultural festival in France. Before reading about the different regions in France and about this regional festival, answer these questions.

1. Do you know about different peoples with different cultures living in the United States?

2. Do they live in particular areas of the country?

3. Do they celebrate their ethnic diversity with festivals? Name some.

4. Locate the following regions on a map of France: *Flandre, Bretagne, Alsace, Gascogne, Languedoc, Roussillon.* Tell in which part of France they are: *au nord, à l'est, au sud, à l'ouest, au nord-est, au sud-ouest,* etc.

Now read the following paragraphs and the festival announcement and do the activities that follow.

La France est un pays qui a assimilé des groupes ethniques très divers: Bretons, Alsaciens, Flamands, Basques, Catalans.

- Les Bretons habitent en Bretagne et sont un peuple d'origine celtique comme les Irlandais; ils parlent la langue bretonne.
- Les Alsaciens habitent au nord-est, en Alsace; ils parlent un dialecte allemand.
- Les Flamands habitent au nord de la France; ils sont d'origine hollandaise et parlent flamand.
- Les Catalans sont descendants de peuples espagnols; ils habitent dans le sud de la France. Ils parlent espagnol, français et catalan.
- Les Basques habitent au sud de la France, dans les montagnes à la frontière entre la France et l'Espagne. Ils parlent basque.

La Fête du Ttorro est un festival de Saint Jean de Luz, une ville où habitent des Basques et des Catalans.

Dimanche 7 SEPTEMBRE

FÊTE DU TTORRO

10 h 30	Animation de la Ville par Txistus et Bandas
12 h 00	Défilé d'enfants costumés
17 h 00	Danses Folkloriques
19 h à 21 h	Concert - Animation par Bandas
19 h 30	GRAND DÎNER en plein air, rue de la République
21 h 30	Place Louis XIV, BAL Bataille de confetti
22 h 30	TORO DE FUEGO
23 h 30	FEUX D'ARTIFICE

ACTIVITÉ 1

1. Reread the announcement and the accompanying paragraphs on cultural and ethnic diversity in France. Then select the statements that most accurately reflect the main idea.
   a. France is a country where only French is spoken.
   b. Several different ethnic groups comprise France today.
   c. There are at least five different languages spoken in France.

2. Make a chart showing the various ethnic groups in France. For each group, list *nom, région, langue* and *origine.*

3. Look at the paragraphs in more detail.
   a. What do the Irish and the Bretons have in common?
   b. Where is a German dialect spoken in France?
   c. Where do they speak Flemish in France?
   d. What two ethnic groups can be found in the south of France?

4. Look at the announcement in more detail. Note that the times are given on a 24-hour clock. When are the following events scheduled?
   a. the children's costume parade
   b. the outdoor dinner
   c. the folk dances
   d. the ball, followed by the confetti battle
   e. the fireworks

5. What would you say is the main purpose of the *Fête du Ttorro?* Is it only to have fun? Is there a cultural goal? What do you think it is?

> **Bonus:** Note that the word *Ttorro* on the advertisement is not spelled in the usual way. Find another spelling on the announcement. The French word is *le taureau.*

Borrowed Words

The announcement uses the words *toro* and *fuego.* The words are not French, but Spanish. Can you think of similar examples of words in another language that are commonly used in English?

During the *danses folkloriques,* participants may dance *la séguedille.* What is that? What is the origin of the word? Find it in a French dictionary. During *le bal,* there will be a *bataille de confetti.* What kind of word is *confetti?* Look it up also.

What about the following French words? Look them up in a French dictionary. Tell what they mean and give their origin.

le bakchich	la mantille
le toubib	le kaiser
le biniou	

Le carnaval de Québec

This schedule announces the events for the winter carnival in Quebec. Before reading it, think about these questions.

1. Make a list of activities that might be scheduled at a winter carnival. Refer to the pictures for some additional ideas.
2. Knowing that the carnival takes place in Canada, think about activities that might reflect the Canadian culture.

Now read the schedule and complete the activities that follow.

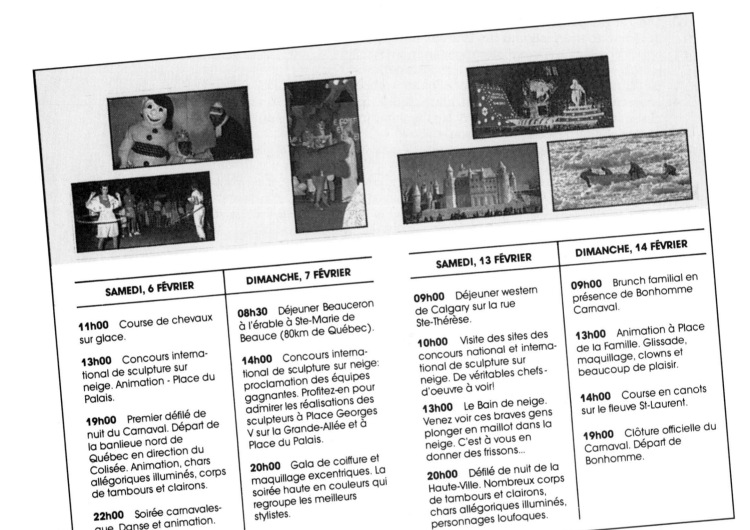

SAMEDI, 6 FÉVRIER	DIMANCHE, 7 FÉVRIER	SAMEDI, 13 FÉVRIER	DIMANCHE, 14 FÉVRIER
11h00 Course de chevaux sur glace.	**08h30** Déjeuner Beauceron à l'érable à Ste-Marie de Beauce (80km de Québec).	**09h00** Déjeuner western de Calgary sur la rue Ste-Thérèse.	**09h00** Brunch familial en présence de Bonhomme Carnaval.
13h00 Concours international de sculpture sur neige. Animation - Place du Palais.	**14h00** Concours international de sculpture sur neige: proclamation des équipes gagnantes. Profitez-en pour admirer les réalisations des sculpteurs à Place Georges V sur la Grande-Allée et à Place du Palais.	**10h00** Visite des sites des concours national et international de sculpture sur neige. De véritables chefs-d'oeuvre à voir!	**13h00** Animation à Place de la Famille. Glissade, maquillage, clowns et beaucoup de plaisir.
19h00 Premier défilé de nuit du Carnaval. Départ de la banlieue nord de Québec en direction du Colisée. Animation, chars allégoriques illuminés, corps de tambours et clairons.		**13h00** Le Bain de neige. Venez voir ces braves gens plonger en maillot dans la neige. C'est à vous en donner des frissons...	**14h00** Course en canots sur le fleuve St-Laurent.
22h00 Soirée carnavalesque. Danse et animation.	**20h00** Gala de coiffure et maquillage excentriques. La soirée haute en couleurs qui regroupe les meilleurs stylistes.	**20h00** Défilé de nuit de la Haute-Ville. Nombreux corps de tambours et clairons, chars allégoriques illuminés, personnages loufoques.	**19h00** Clôture officielle du Carnaval. Départ de Bonhomme.

ACTIVITÉ 2

Reread the schedule of events, then answer these questions.

1. Which of the following statements best summarizes the schedule?
   a. There are many varied activities during a winter carnival in Quebec.
   b. Carnivals generally offer very few fun activities.
   c. This carnival is primarily for adults.
2. Look carefully at the schedule to find these specific pieces of information.
   a. During what month does the carnival take place?
   b. Is the carnival scheduled on weekdays or on weekends?
   c. Are the hours the same on Saturday and Sunday? from one weekend to the next?
   d. Which day offers the greatest number of activities?
   e. On which day(s) does the schedule begin with breakfast?
   f. On what day and at what time is the dance scheduled?
   g. When do the snow sculpture events take place?
   h. When does the boat race take place?
   i. When does the carnival end?

BONUS: What is the name of the carnival mascot? What does he look like?

Borrowed Words

The carnival schedule uses the words *western* and *brunch.* The words are not French, but English. They are good examples of borrowed words, which occur frequently in Canadian French. The borrowed words are used to describe events that have no equivalent in French. For instance, there is no single word to describe a late breakfast in French. The English word *brunch* is therefore borrowed. Since French does not have a way to describe a "western" breakfast, using the English word most appropriately describes the event.

Look for another English word used in French in the schedule. Hint: it occurs in the listing for Sunday, February 14 at 1 p.m.

NOTES CULTURELLES

There are many festivals in France throughout the year. Film festivals such as *le Festival de Cannes* provide an opportunity to see the latest films. Dance festivals such as *le Festival International de Danse de Paris* allow dancers to show their skills. Music, art, and folk festivals are also quite common and are joyous celebrations of the various arts.

PRO**J**ETS

1. Do you know of anyone with an interesting cultural or ethnic background? Ask your classmates if they know of anyone with a special history. What is that person's ethnic origin? Find out how to say it in French by using your French-English dictionary. Also look up the place of origin of that ethnic group in an atlas. Where do most people in your class come from? Europe? Asia? Africa?

2. Draw up a schedule for a carnival similar to the one in Quebec. Be sure to include interesting and fun activities.

3. Plan a festival or carnival for your class.

À L'ORAL

Look at the events scheduled for both festivals described in this chapter. Select an event and invite a friend to go with you. Your friend should ask what time the event is scheduled. Then switch roles.

—*Tu veux aller au concert?*
—*À quelle heure est le concert?*
—*Il est à 19 heures.*
—...

C H A P I T R E   1 0

TU VOUDRAIS ALLER EN VILLE AVEC MOI?

1. There are many different ways to get around town. Identify the types of transportation that are shown in the photograph.

On peut aller…

à pied	en métro	en train
en avion	en voiture	en moto
en bateau	en mobylette	en bus
en taxi		

2. What safety precautions do you notice in the photograph?

- Quel moyen de transport préférez-vous? —*Je préfère aller…*
- Comment allez-vous à l'école? —*Je vais à l'école…*

Mon Rapido

This advertisement for a scooter has been adapted from a French magazine. Before reading it, think about these questions.

1. Did you know that there are no school buses in France and that one must be 18 years old to drive a car alone? Make a list of the means of transportation French students might use to get to school.

2. Which are the most economical means of transportation? Which are the fastest?

Now look at the picture, read the advertisement, and do the activities that follow.

MÊME A FOND LE RAPIDO FAIT MOINS DE BRUIT QU'UNE GIBSON, MAIS POUR LES BALLADES EN SOLO IL VA PLUS LOIN...

Le Rapido est un scooter de 50cc pour les jeunes, pour les fanatiques de rock. Il nous entraîne partout en ville sans permis de conduire, même à 14 ans. Moderne comme le rock, il a un démarreur électrique, des roues en aluminium et une transmission automatique. Il nous transporte loin avec son grand réservoir plein de super.

ACTIVITÉ 1

1. Reread the passage, then choose the statement that best summarizes it.
   a. In this advertisement, the Rapido scooter is described as a modern means of transportation for young people.
   b. In this advertisement, the ecological importance of driving a motorcycle is stressed.
   c. The text describes the disadvantages of driving a car in a highly congested area.

2. Advertisements are usually directed toward a particular group.
   a. What age group does this advertisement address?
   b. Why would the advertisers put a guitar in the ad?
   c. How old do you need to be to drive a Rapido?
   d. Do you need a driver's license?

3. Tell whether the following statements are *vrai* or *faux*. Correct the false ones.
   a. The Rapido has an electric starter so that you can turn it on with a key.
   b. The Rapido is a solid, heavy machine with steel wheels.
   c. The Rapido features an automatic transmission.
   d. The Rapido will travel only short distances because of its small fuel tank.
   e. The Rapido runs on electricity.

BONUS: The advertiser compares the Rapido to a Gibson guitar. What similarities does the advertisement suggest? what differences?

4. Read each description, then tell if it represents an advantage or a disadvantage of owning a scooter. Are there any statements that you believe are untrue?
   a. Ce n'est pas cher à acheter.
   b. Il fait très froid en hiver.
   c. C'est pratique.
   d. C'est facile à stationner.
   e. C'est moderne comme le rock.
   f. C'est dangereux.
   g. C'est amusant.
   h. C'est économique.
   i. Ce n'est pas confortable.
   j. On n'a pas besoin d'un permis.

5. Would you like to own a scooter? Be prepared to justify your response.

Locating the Topic Sentence

Topic sentences state the main idea of a paragraph. They are usually found at or near the beginning of each paragraph in the passage. This is, however, not always the case.

1. Carefully reread the scooter advertisement.
   a. Find the sentence that sums up or explains what was said in all of the other sentences.
   b. Compare your choice of sentence with that of your classmates. In your collective opinion, which is the topic sentence of the passage?
   c. Why do you think the writers of the ad placed the topic sentence in this position in the paragraph?

2. Imagine that you were invited to write one-paragraph advertisements for a scooter or mini-bike, a luxury or touring cycle, and a rallye or off-road bike. Prepare two topic sentences for each kind of bike.

3. Look back at the statements in question 4. Write a topic sentence about the advantages or disadvantages of driving a scooter. Then select from those statements the ones that support your point.

La sécurité en moto

The following article on motorcycle safety is from the magazine *Phosphore*. Before reading this article, compare the rider in the line drawing with the one in the photograph.

1. Why do you think the rider in the photograph has chosen to go without a helmet? Would you make the same decision? Be prepared to explain why.

2. Read over the title, the subtitle, and the four sentences in large type above the picture.

    a. On the basis of this preview, what do you think the text will be about?

    b. Does this introduction to the passage explain why the rider in the photograph is not wearing a helmet?

    c. What contrast does this introductory paragraph make between movies and real life?

    d. What point do you think the author is trying to make by contrasting the appearance of the cycle-riding movie actor with that of the ordinary cycle rider?

Now read the remainder of the article and do the activities that follow.

AUTO MOTO-PHOSPHORE

MOTO
Le casque ou la vie

A moto ou à cyclo, la sécurité passe d'abord par le casque. Et ce n'est pas parce que les héros de cinéma ou de télévision l'oublient souvent qu'il faut les imiter. Car à la télévision, après un accident, le film continue. Tandis que dans la vie...

Voici la réponse:
Un casque, évidemment. Mais tous les jeunes ne savent pas qu'il est obligatoire de porter un casque.

La preuve:
- Il y a trop d'infractions chaque année.
- On dit que plus de 11% des pilotes de cyclomoteur ou de motocyclette refusent de «s'alourdir la tête».

Le savez-vous?
Les policiers et gendarmes ont dressé plus de 75 739 procès-verbaux en 1988. Pour quelle infraction?

Vous ne savez pas?
Alors: qu'est-ce qui est rond comme un ballon et obligatoire depuis 1976 pour les pilotes de cyclomoteur ou de motocyclette?

Par conséquent:
- Il y a 11% d'inconscients qui négligent les nécessités de la sécurité.
- Il y a 11% qui ne veulent pas tenir compte d'une statistique indiscutable: avec un casque, le risque de se tuer en cas d'accident est divisé par deux.

ACTIVITÉ 2

1. Quickly read over the passage again, then choose the main idea from among the statements that follow.
   a. This article presents statistical evidence in support of wearing a motorcycle helmet.
   b. The passage explains how motorcycle helmets are designed to protect the rider.
   c. The text focuses on the do's and don'ts of motorcycle ownership.
2. In 1988 how many tickets were written to cycle riders who did not obey the mandatory helmet law?
3. Since what year has it been mandatory to wear a motorcycle helmet in France?
4. What proof does the article provide to show that all cycle riders do not wear helmets?

5. Why, according to the article, do cycle riders refuse to wear helmets?
6. By what percentage does wearing a helmet reduce one's risk of death in case of an accident?
7. Do you find this article convincing? Why or why not?

BONUS: According to the article, there is a difference between an actor in a movie not wearing a helmet and a person in real traffic not wearing one. What is it?

Finding Supporting Details

Topic sentences are usually reinforced and explained in one of several ways.
- With specific details and illustrations
- With anecdotes or stories from the writer's personal experience
- With statistics and other data from a documented and reliable source

1. How does the writer of the article reinforce and explain the topic sentence in this passage?
2. Does the writer's choice of supporting statistical details make the article more convincing, or do these details make the passage less believable?
3. How would the article be different if, instead of using statistical data, the writer had:
   a. not supported his topic sentence with any details at all?
   b. related personal experiences to support his point?
   c. cited examples from television, cinema, or literature?

NOTES CULTURELLES

Read over the following information on the different kinds of driving permits for motorcycles and cars for which one might choose to qualify in France.

PERMIS DE CONDUIRE	CATÉGORIES DE VÉHICULES	AGE MINIMUM
A1	Motocyclettes de 1ère catégorie, plus de 50 cm³ sans excéder 80 cm³, vitesse limitée par construction à 75 km/h	16 ans
A2	Motocyclettes de 2e catégorie, plus de 80 cm³ sans excéder 400 cm³	18 ans
A3	Motocyclettes de 3e catégorie, plus de 400 cm³	18 ans
A4	Tricycles et quadricycles à moteur, n'excédant pas 125 cm³	16 ans
B	Véhicules affectés du transport de personnes ou de marchandises, ne dépassant pas 3,5 tonne et comportant 8 places assises au maximum, siège du conducteur non compris.	18 ans

PROJETS

1. Is there a helmet law in your state? How do you feel about the presence or absence of such a law?
   a. State your opinion in a short topic sentence.
   b. Support your point of view with two examples.
   c. Summarize your position in a brief concluding remark.
2. Contact your local licence bureau and obtain information about special permits for three- and four-wheelers, scooters, and motorcycles. Compare the American laws with the French ones above.

À L'ORAL

Interview your partner, using the following opening questions and others of your choice. Change roles.

—Avez-vous un vélo (une bicyclette)?
—Avez-vous une mobylette ou une moto?
—Si vous avez un vélo, une mobylette ou une moto, portez-vous un casque?
—...

PRENONS LE MÉTRO!

Test your métro knowledge!

1. A series of stations along a route serviced in sequence by a train is called:
   a. a destination   b. a line   c. a queue

2. Routes in the Paris métro are named according to:
   a. the stations at each end of the line
   b. the largest station along the line
   c. the first station where two lines intersect

3. A métro station located at the intersection of two lines, at which passengers can change from one line to another, is called:
   a. a switchover   b. a crossing   c. a *correspondance*

4. Although the métro does not serve the suburbs of Paris directly, most of the end stations are linked to another system of train transportation called:
   a. the R.E.R.   b. the S.N.C.F.   c. the R.A.T.P.

5. One can purchase all of the following types of métro tickets except a:
   a. single-ride ticket   b. booklet *(un carnet)* of 10 tickets
   c. weekly pass   d. monthly pass   e. yearly pass

6. In the Paris métro, ticket prices:
   a. depend on the distance traveled, with longer trips costing more
   b. cost more as one gets closer to the center of Paris
   c. are the same for all destinations within the métro system and include connections to the R.E.R. without an increase in fare

Answers: 1b, 2a, 3c, 4a, 5e, 6c

Les robots du métro

There are several subheadings in the following news item from the magazine *Ça va*. In Chapter 7 we focused on using titles, headings, and subheadings to determine what a passage will be about. Skim the title and headings in the following text, then tell in which section you might find information about:

1. What happens when the cleaning personnel go on strike
2. A futuristic solution to the problem
3. What the travelers leave behind

Now read the article and do the activities that follow.

Une montagne d'ordures

Les voyageurs du métro à Paris sont très nombreux. Il y a plus d'un million de voyageurs par jour; ils parcourent les 57 kilomètres de couloirs du métro et emploient toutes les stations du réseau. Ils laissent aussi une montagne d'ordures dans le métro. Heureusement il y a 1 500 balayeurs pour nettoyer.

Les grèves de nettoyeurs

De temps en temps il y a des grèves des nettoyeurs. Par exemple, en 1977 et en 1980 les balayeurs ont fait la grève. Et

Pardon, Madame

les ordures se sont accumulées: des tonnes d'ordures, des odeurs, des rats, des grands dangers hygiéniques.

La solution: les robots-nettoyeurs

La Régie Autonome des Transports Parisiens (R.A.T.P.) qui se charge de l'administration du métro a décidé de trouver une solution. La R.A.T.P. veut remplacer les balayeurs avec des robots-nettoyeurs.
Dans quelques années 500 robots-nettoyeurs vont remplacer les balayeurs du métro. Ces robots vont nettoyer les quais, les couloirs et même les trains et les tunnels.

ACTIVITÉ 1

1. Quickly reread the passage, then choose the best summary.
   a. There is a mountain of garbage in the métro, and nothing can be done about it.
   b. Robots designed to clean the métro will be used in the near future.
   c. Most of the hygienic problems in the métro stem from rats.

2. Reread the article and answer the following questions.
   a. How many travelers are there every day in the métro?
   b. How many kilometers of corridors are there?
   c. How many sweepers are employed?
   d. Have there ever been sweeper strikes? If so, when?
   e. What happens during a sweeper strike?
   f. How many robots do they intend to build?
   g. What specific tasks will the robots have?

BONUS: What might the robot say to people waiting for the métro train? What do you think people might answer?

3. Select from among the following sentences those that reflect your opinion about the robots in the métro. Practice with a friend asking and answering the question, «*Qu'est-ce que tu penses des robots du métro?*»
   —*Une solution est nécessaire.*
   —*La R.A.T.P. a raison.*
   —*Une machine compliquée comme le robot ne marche pas toujours.*
   —*Les balayeurs sont importants.*
   —*Les ordures ne sont pas hygiéniques.*
   —*Les robots-nettoyeurs sont une solution moderne.*
   —*Les robots-nettoyeurs sont très chers.*

Outlining

Outlining is a system for identifying and organizing topic sentences and supporting details. Outlines often follow this format:

Title
   I. Main point
      A. Supporting information
      B. Additional supporting information
      C. …
   II. Second main point
      A. …
   III. …

Often, main headings in a text directly reflect the main points represented by the roman numerals in the outline. Details that support the main point are developed directly from the information indicated by capital letters.

   In the following list, the title, main headings, and supporting facts of the robot article have been jumbled. Reconstruct the outline of the article by rearranging the items in outline form.

il y a 1 500 balayeurs
des tonnes d'ordures
La solution: les robots-nettoyeurs
les robots vont remplacer les balayeurs
LES ROBOTS DU MÉTRO
Les grèves de nettoyeurs
en 1977 et en 1980 les balayeurs ont fait la grève
La R.A.T.P. a décidé de trouver une solution
Une montagne d'ordures
500 robots

Un centre commercial

Before reading this article from *Paris Magazine*, focus on the key word in the title: *souk*. A *souk* is a bazaar, or a popular shopping area. The word is borrowed from Arabic.

1. What do you think a *souk souterrain* might refer to? Where might it be located?

2. Scan the main headings. What types of information do you think you will gain from reading this article?

Now read the article and do the activities that follow.

LE SOUK SOUTERRAIN

Un mégacentre commercial

Le métro n'est plus un désert. La R.A.T.P. est en train de transformer ses couloirs et ses quais en mégacentre commercial où on trouve tout. Marchands des quatre saisons, compagnie d'assurances, banque, pharmacie, cafétérias, coiffeurs, librairies, agences de voyages, auto-école, vêtements,... plus de cinq cent boutiques qui offrent un service express au voyageur.

Un shopping spécialisé

S'il existe des boutiques et des services dans le réseau du métro, c'est pour faciliter la vie des deux millions de voyageurs qui utilisent ses couloirs chaque jour. On ne fait pas le shopping dans le métro, mais c'est l'occasion qui crée le consommateur souterrain. Les boutiques sont ouvertes les jours de semaine et tout spécialement autour des horaires 7h-9h et 17h-19h. Il s'agit donc d'un shopping d'avant et d'après le travail.

Une grande variété de boutiques

Il y a 107 magasins de développement photo, 82 bijouteries, 40 boutiques de prêt-à-porter, 34 cordonneries minute, 31 cafétérias et 28 magasins de produits de beauté. Il y a aussi des boutiques spécialisées: banque, jouets, fourrures, agence immobilière, auto-école.

Pour un cadeau de dernière minute, quand on n'a pas le temps de faire ses courses, c'est idéal!

ACTIVITÉ 2

1. Quickly reread the passage, then choose the sentence that best sums up the main idea.
   a. The métro is becoming more than just a system of public transportation.
   b. Many people shop in the métro because of the large number of stores and the extended hours.
   c. The shops are generally expensive and luxurious.
2. The author provides information on the number and types of stores and services in two places in the passage.
   a. How many stores are there?
   b. Name the different types of stores.
   c. What products or services could you obtain in each one?
   d. Which types of stores are most frequently represented?
3. Analyze the marketing philosophy that has resulted in such a *mégacentre commercial.*

   a. How do stores justify their presence in a public transportation system?
   b. What are the store hours?
   c. How do the hours of operation reflect this philosophy?
4. Reread the first paragraph and locate its topic sentence.
5. Reread the entire text to find a concluding sentence—that is, a sentence that sums up the whole article.
6. What shops are shown in the photograph? Are these stores that you would be likely to visit?

BONUS: What is the R.A.T.P.? Hint: Look in the previous reading in this chapter.

Outlining

Outlining is an easy way of structuring information before communicating it to someone else as well as a simple means of understanding how a text you are reading is organized. To better understand the passage *Le souk souterrain,* outline it for yourself using the outline skeleton begun below.

Le souk souterrain
  I. La R.A.T.P. transforme le métro en mégacentre commercial avec plus de 500 boutiques.
     A. les marchands des quatre saisons
     B. ...
     ...
  II. Les boutiques existent pour...
     A. ...
     ...
  III. ...
     ...
     ...

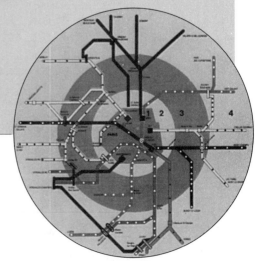

NOTES CULTURELLES

Le trafic voyageurs de la R.A.T.P.

(millions de voyageurs)	
Métropolitain	1 176
R.E.R.	292
Ensemble du réseau routier	760
TOTAL	2 228

Le métro

La première ligne de métro a été inaugurée pour l'Exposition universelle de 1900. Le réseau comprend aujourd'hui 15 lignes totalisant 198 kilomètres. Le système est simple et pratique: les trains sont très fréquents et s'arrêtent à toutes les stations.

Les autobus et les taxis

Cinquante-six lignes d'autobus totalisent 518 km et plus de 1 600 arrêts. Par ailleurs, 14 300 taxis effectuent environ 165 000 courses quotidiennes. Malheureusement, il n'y a jamais assez de taxis aux heures de pointe.

PROJETS

1. Prepare a newspaper advertisement for a new branch of a store or office located underground along the métro; be sure to include your address, métro stop(s), directions from major points within the city, hours of operation, and services.
2. Draw a sample shopping corridor in a métro station; label each place of business. Write a short description of this portion of the shopping center. Note the relationships among the different buildings (*le café Voltaire est en face de la banque, etc.*).
3. In English, write a paragraph explaining how you think the use of robots will change your life in the future.

À L'ORAL

Discuss with a partner your transportation preferences. Tell what means of transportation you use for various activities.

—*Quand je vais ...*
  à l'école
  au cinéma
  au match de football
  en pique-nique
  en voyage
...je vais...
  à pied
  en voiture
  en taxi
  en métro
  en autobus.
Et toi?
—*Moi, quand je vais...*

CHAPITRE 12

ON VA À PIED? ONON!

This photograph was taken at a recent auto show in France. The cars you see were available for sale that year.

1. What kinds of cars are they? How do they differ from American cars? Consider size, sportiness, and style in your answer.

2. Would you buy one of the cars in the photograph? Tell why or why not.

BONUS: The names of two automobile manufacturers are only partially visible in the photograph. Can you tell what the names are? What other French car makers are you familiar with?

Une belle voiture

The following advertisement comes from the French magazine *Match*. It discusses features that one should look for when buying a car. What would you look for in a car? Arrange the following features in descending order of importance.

Je voudrais une voiture...

___ économique

___ nerveuse *(peppy)*

___ bien équipée *(well-equipped)*

___ maniable et compacte *(maneuverable)*

___ fiable *(reliable)*

___ à 5 vitesses *(speeds)*

___ rouge

Now read the ad and do the activities that follow.

1) M. Lebec. 2) La Corolla de M. Lebec, une confortable voiture de route. 3) Mme Lebec. 4) La Corolla de Mme Lebec, une petite voiture de ville maniable. 5) Le petit Luc. Monsieur Lebec est vétérinaire près de Rouen, jeune vétérinaire. Il voyage fréquemment dans la région. Il choisit pour cela une voiture bien équipée, moteur 1,3 litres, et 5 vitesses; c'est-à-dire fiable, nerveuse et économique.

Madame Lebec est la femme de Monsieur Lebec; elle fait ses courses à Rouen et elle choisit une voiture maniable et compacte car elle fréquente aussi les brocantes. Le petit Luc, lui ne choisit rien. Il veut une voiture rouge. Monsieur Lebec est très content de sa voiture et Madame Lebec aussi. De temps en temps Monsieur Lebec emprunte la voiture de sa femme pour aller en ville, et lorsque Madame Lebec va visiter une brocante, elle prend la voiture de son mari. Le petit Luc ne comprend pas très bien cette distinction; il ne voit pas clairement la différence entre la Corolla Hatchback de son papa et la Corolla Hatchback de sa maman; mais c'est sans doute parce qu'il est petit.

GARANTIE TOYOTA **3** ANS OU 100000 KM

TOYOTA

MA TOYOTA EST FANTASTIQUE

ACTIVITÉ 1

1. Read quickly through the passage again, then choose the sentence below that best summarizes the main idea of the Corolla ad.
   a. Each member of the family sees the Corolla as a different car.
   b. Mrs. Lebec sees the car as a compact luxury car.
   c. Mr. Lebec sees his car as a well-equipped highway car.
   d. Luc Lebec likes red cars.
   e. The main thing is that the car is fast.

2. This advertisement focuses on perceptions. Mr. Lebec perceives the car differently from Mrs. Lebec or Luc Lebec. Find the features that Mr. Lebec, Mrs. Lebec, and Luc Lebec look for in a car and list them under each of their names.

3. Sometimes Mr. Lebec needs the features for which Mrs. Lebec chose the car. Sometimes Mrs. Lebec needs the features for which her husband chose the car. Find in the text the situations when each needs the other's features, and complete the sentences below. What does Luc Lebec think of all of this?

   a. M. Lebec veut...
   b. Mme Lebec veut...
   c. M. Lebec veut de temps en temps...
   d. Mme Lebec veut de temps en temps...
   e. Luc Lebec pense...

4. Read each description and select the features of the car you would choose under the three different conditions. Work with a partner.

   économique   compacte
   confortable   fiable
   maniable   à 5 vitesses
   nerveuse   rouge
   bien équipée

   a. Je suis M. Lebec; je suis vétérinaire. Je voyage fréquemment dans la région. J'ai besoin d'une voiture...
   b. Je suis Mme Lebec; je fais des courses à Rouen et je fréquente les brocantes. Je voudrais une voiture...
   c. Je suis Luc Lebec. Je voudrais une Corolla...

Taking Notes

Are you a transcriber or an efficient notetaker? Here's how to tell.
- If you try to get down every word, copying word for word what a speaker says, you are a transcriber.
- If you listen and record in your own words key phrases, main ideas, supporting examples, summary statements, and occasional key terms, definitions, and examples to clarify those ideas, you are a notetaker.

Effective notetaking is an art — the art of sifting, summarizing, and recording information for future reference and review. Practice your note-taking skills in the following manner: Listen as your teacher, a classmate, or your partner reads the first paragraph of the car ad. Don't try to take down every word. Instead, jot down some key words and phrases. Afterwards link them together in a single statement of the main idea that will remind you how those phrases fit together.

Bons et mauvais conducteurs

People from different regions of the country often have different reputations as drivers. For instance, New York cab drivers are reputed to have a short temper and to drive without much regard for the rules of the road. The following article from the French magazine *Phosphore* rates drivers from different European countries. Before reading the article, think about these questions.

1. Think of drivers from various regions. Do any of them have a reputation of being especially courteous?
2. Are there any who have the reputation of being especially aggressive?
3. Do any exceed speed limits regularly?

Now read the article and do the activities that follow.

conduire: *to drive*
se conduire: *to behave*

AUTO MOTO-PHOSPHORE

EUROPE
Comment (se) conduisent nos voisins?

Beaucoup de Français croient qu'ils sont des as du volant.

Le gentleman conducteur

Les automobilistes britanniques jouent fair play, ils respectent les règles de la route plus que les Français. Le résultat est qu'il y a deux fois moins de tués en Angleterre qu'en France. La courtoisie influe certainement sur le comportement du conducteur anglais: il s'arrête automatiquement pour laisser passer les piétons, il remercie souvent l'automobiliste qui le laisse passer et ne perd pas son sang-froid.

Code plus discipliné

En Allemagne on respecte les limitations de vitesse sur les routes. Très prudents sur les routes, les Allemands n'hésitent pas de foncer à 200 km/h sur leurs autoroutes, les seules en Europe sans limitation.

Vous avez dit audace?

Il y a une manière latine de conduire. Une fois de l'autre côté des Alpes ou des Pyrénées, les règles ne sont pas tout à fait les mêmes. Les panneaux de limitation de vitesse deviennent moins importants. La loi, c'est souvent la loi du plus courageux. L'Espagnol et l'Italien ont une perception du risque bien différente que chez les Allemands. Étonnant, non?

ACTIVITÉ 2

1. Reread the passage and then tell which sentence most accurately summarizes it.
   a. Documentation in this article shows that the French are the best drivers in Europe.
   b. Drivers from different countries don't all show the same respect for the rules of the road.
   c. The article focuses on different driving laws and regulations in European countries.

2. Which of these opinions are supported by the article?
   a. The French consider themselves driving champions, but statistics do not show this.
   b. German drivers are more respectful of driving regulations.
   c. Spanish and Italian drivers are not very careful.
   d. British drivers are the worst.

3. Look at the details in the article and match the drivers with their habits.

Les Français...
Les Allemands...
Les Britanniques...
Les Espagnols et les Italiens...

   a. respectent les limitations de vitesse.
   b. sont les plus courageux.
   c. ont une perception différente du risque.
   d. jouent fair play.
   e. n'hésitent pas de foncer sur l'autoroute.
   f. considèrent les panneaux de vitesse moins importants.
   g. ne perdent pas le sang-froid.

4. Of the drivers discussed in the article, which are the safest, in your opinion?

BONUS: The article mentions a speed limit of 200 km per hour on the Autobahn in Germany. How many miles per hour is that?

Taking Notes

To be an efficient notetaker, you must develop the skill of deciding which are the most important things to take down. For instance, theme sentences are more important than examples. The following suggestions can help you to improve your notes:

1. Take down main titles and headings. These are the main divisions in what is said or written.
2. Write action verbs and their complements. Avoid writing negative sentences or questions.
3. Limit the number of examples to two; choose the best ones.
4. Use short sentences in a telegraphic style. Do not try to take down every word or to copy whole sentences. Simplify.

Read the article on European drivers once more. Take notes on one or more paragraphs as you read. Follow some of the suggestions given above. After you have taken notes, try to reconstruct the passage. How close did you come to giving the important points? Does your reconstruction make sense? Is it too short, too sketchy? Are you satisfied with it?

NOTES CULTURELLES

Le permis de conduire en France

According to French law, young people cannot get a driver's license until they are 18 years of age and have completed courses in an approved driving school. Driver training is not provided in French high schools. Driver training courses tend to be expensive, and it is difficult to obtain a driver's license on the first attempt.

There is, however, a legal way to drive at 16 or 17 in France. You can join a program called *la conduite accompagnée*. To join, you must first take 20 hours of instruction in a driving school, where you learn about the basic parts of the car, such as its engine and transmission, lights, etc. Then, if all goes well, you may be able to drive with a licensed driver (generally a parent). When you turn 18, you will be able to drive alone. However, during the first few months after getting your license, you will be restricted to 90 km

À L'ORAL

Tell why you like (or would like) to drive. Use the French words and expressions below to write one or more sentences. Add your own reasons.

—J'aime (j'aimerais) conduire parce que...
   c'est amusant
   c'est pratique
   c'est plus rapide que
    d'aller à pied
   on peut inviter ses amis
   on peut aller où on veut
   c'est confortable
   on peut aller quand on
    veut
   on peut visiter d'autres
    villes...

This reminder that drinking and driving are a lethal combination is taken from a popular Canadian teen magazine.

PROJETS

1. Inquire about state regulations concerning when you can drive. What is the minimum age? What are the requirements for driving? Are there restrictions for certain conditions such as poor vision? Can you get a learner's permit? Is there a mandatory vehicle inspection before you can drive a vehicle? Is there a seatbelt law?

2. Design your own car and prepare an ad for it. Use the ad in this chapter as a model.

C H A P I T R E   1 3

AH BON, TU VEUX CONNAÎTRE PARIS!

Paris is a city with many faces. Do you recognize this building? In 1971, Georges Pompidou, then *Président de la République*, decided to have a national art and cultural center built in Paris. This ultramodern museum, completed in January 1977, reflects all aspects of communication and the arts. The *Centre culturel* at Beaubourg has elicited strong reactions—positive and negative. It has been described as both a petroleum refinery and a great work of contemporary art!

1. What is your opinion of this style of architecture?
2. What kinds of art works (ceramics, painting, sculpture…), styles (classical, Impressionist, abstract…), and artists do you prefer?
3. What type of art would you expect to be exhibited at the *Centre culturel*?

The *Centre culturel* at Beaubourg is only one of many places to visit in and around Paris. Turn the page to find out about several others.

Les excursions en autobus

These descriptions of day tours in and around Paris were taken from a brochure. Before reading them, spend a few minutes with a partner making an itinerary.

1. Make a list of the kinds of activities and sights that are available in a big city like Paris and that one could not find in smaller towns and rural areas.

2. Work with a partner to answer the following question:

   —*Où veux-tu aller?*

   —*Moi, je préfère visiter la Tour Eiffel / le Louvre / les Champs-Élysées...*

3. Prioritize your list to indicate your preferences. Compare your list with those of several classmates, or make a class profile to determine which activities and sights are the most popular.

Now read the brochure descriptions and do the activities that follow.

PARIS

Vous allez faire une excursion en autobus, dans un autobus des années 1930. Vous allez découvrir les plus beaux lieux de la capitale: Madeleine, Concorde, Champs-Élysées, Arc de Triomphe, Trocadéro, Tour Eiffel, Champs de Mars, École Militaire, UNESCO, Invalides, Quai de Seine, Cité, Notre Dame, Hôtel de Ville, Place des Vosges, Bastille, rue Saint-Antoine, rue de Rivoli, Palais Royal, Opéra. Ce circuit comprend également une promenade en bateau sur la Seine.

DATES

Tous les dimanches du 6 mai au 26 août.

Départ à 13 h 30. Retour vers 18 h 00.

PRIX 175 F

PRIX RÉDUIT 140 F

PARC ASTÉRIX

Le parc de loisirs autour d'Astérix, héros sympathique, mondialement connu, est une excursion idéale. Il y a plus de 100 divertissements, attractions et manèges, spectacles vivants, automates, vieux métiers, reconstitutions, animaux savants, restauration, boutiques, dans le cadre de cinq mondes différents.

DATES

Mercredi 2 mai. Mercredi 16 mai. Mercredi 6 juin. Mercredi 20 juin. Mercredi 4 juillet. Mercredi 18 juillet. Mercredi 1er août. Mercredi 15 août. Mercredi 5 septembre.

Départ à 12 h 30. Retour vers 19 h 00.

PRIX 175 F

PRIX RÉDUIT 140 F

GIVERNY

Vous allez découvrir la maison et les jardins de Claude Monet. C'est la maison où il a vécu entre 1883 et 1926. Vous allez visiter les jardins, l'atelier et aussi les pièces de la maison. Les jardins sont très beaux, avec une allée centrale, le «jardin d'eau», le pont japonais, des arbres et des fleurs.

DATES

Tous les samedis du 5 mai au 13 octobre inclus.

Départ à 13 h. Retour vers 18 h 30.

PRIX 150 F

PRIX RÉDUIT 120 F

Programme et tarif différents les 1er samedi de chaque mois.

Plus de
100 excursions
pour varier vos horizons

Les Bus DÉCOUVERTE

EXTRAITS DU PROGRAMME EXCURSIONS

CHAPITRE 13

/

ACTIVITÉ 1

1. Scan the announcements, then choose the best summary.
  a. This company specializes in bus tours.
  b. The tours offered in this brochure include sights in and around Paris.
  c. This company offers historic, artistic, touristic, and amusement tours.
2. Which tour takes place in a special bus? Describe this vehicle and the tour.
3. Reread the description of Giverny.
  a. Who is associated with Giverny?
  b. Are Monet's paintings displayed there in a museum?
  c. Which portions of the property are included on the tour of Giverny?
4. Reread the description of the Parc Astérix.
  a. What kind of park is described?
  b. What events and activities are offered?
  c. When are the tours scheduled?
5. Consider the details of the proposed tours.
  a. Which tour is the most expensive? the least? Are there discount prices?
  b. Although the sites are open on other days of the week, bus tours are proposed only on certain days. Which tour is offered on Sundays? Wednesdays? Saturdays? Are the sites open year round?

Which has the longest season? Why is this particularly appropriate?
  c. Are the tours scheduled for morning or afternoon departures? What is the approximate length of the visits? Which is the longest?

BONUS: Do you know why tour visits are scheduled for the Parc Astérix only on Wednesday? Hint: When do you think French students have a day off?

6. Prepare a guided tour for one of the sites, using this model.
Vous aimez ____? Alors, visitez ____! Vous allez voir____ et vous allez certainement aimer____. Le départ est à ____ Le prix réduit de l'excursion est ____!

Insert the following information:
  a. *Paris / la ville en autobus / les monuments / la Tour Eiffel / 13h 30 / 140F*
  b. *Monet / Giverny / les jardins / le pont japonais / 13h / 120F*
  c. *Astérix / le parc Astérix / les spectacles / les automates / 12h 30 / 140F*

Types of Texts

Authors write different materials for different occasions and reasons. Identifying the type of text and understanding its purpose are essential to understanding the text itself.
1. Brainstorm with a partner, in a small group, or with your class about the different types of material that are produced in writing. What kinds of printed material do you, your parents, and others read during an ordinary day?
2. Now think about the different purposes each kind of text seeks to accomplish. Here is the beginning of such a list.
Writers write to:
  a. describe
  b. inform/explain
  c. report/narrate/tell a story
  d. entertain/amuse
  e. convince/persuade
  Add to the list as many additional purposes as you can.
3. What do you think is the purpose of this bus tour brochure?

Les Champs-Élysées

The Champs-Élysées is the most famous avenue in Paris. The Champs-Élysées offers spectacular views of some of the most famous sites in the city. Look closely at the map. Locate the Rond Point, then look up and down the avenue to find each of the sites and views described.

1. From the Rond Point, look up the avenue toward the Arc de Triomphe.

2. From the Rond Point, look down the avenue:

    a. past the *Place de la Concorde*, site of the 3,300-year-old obelisk from the ruins of the temple at Luxor

    b. into the *Jardin des Tuileries*, the very elegant formal gardens

    c. through the smaller *Arc de Triomphe du Carousel*

    d. into the courtyard of the Louvre, one of the world's great museums

me baladais: *was walking*
suffisait de: *was enough to*
t'apprivoiser: *to tame you*
ce fut toi: *it was you*

Now read the lyrics of the song *Les Champs-Élysées* and do the activities that follow.

Les Champs-Élysées—Joe Dassin

Je me baladais sur l'avenue
Le cœur ouvert à l'inconnu.
J'avais envie de dire «bon-
    jour»
À n'importe qui.
N'importe qui, et ce fut toi.
Je t'ai dit n'importe quoi.
Il suffisait de te parler
Pour t'apprivoiser.

REFRAIN

Aux Champs-Élysées
Aux Champs-Élysées
Au soleil, sous la pluie
À midi ou à minuit
Il y a tout ce que vous
    voulez
Aux Champs-Élysées.

Tu m'as dit «J'ai rendez-vous
Dans un sous-sol avec des
    fous
Qui vivent la guitare à la main
Du soir au matin.»
Alors je t'ai accompagnée
On a chanté, on a dansé
Et on n'a même pas pensé
À s'embrasser.

REFRAIN

Hier soir, deux inconnus
Et ce matin sur l'avenue
Deux amoureux tout étourdis
Par la longue nuit.
Et de l'Étoile à la Concorde
Un orchestre à mille cordes
Tous les oiseaux du point du
    jour
Chantent l'amour.

REFRAIN

ACTIVITÉ 2

1. Scan the song, then select the best summary.
   a. The Champs-Élysées offers everything in the way of amusements and entertainment that one could ever want.
   b. There is always something happening on the Champs-Élysées, no matter who you are, what the weather, or what time of day.
   c. The Champs-Élysées is a street where people meet and get acquainted.

2. Reread the lyrics, then select as many answers as are correct:
   a. Where was the singer at the time of this rendez-vous?
      — au café
      — sur l'avenue
      — à la Concorde
   b. Whom did he meet?
      — une ancienne amie
      — une nouvelle amie
      — sa soeur

   c. Where did they go?
      — dans un sous-sol
      — à l'Étoile
      — au Louvre
   d. What did they do?
      — on a mangé
      — on a chanté
      — on a visité l'Étoile
   e. After spending the evening together, they:
      — never saw each other
      — fell in love
      — went walking on the Champs-Élysées again

3. Read the lyrics again and find the lines in the first two stanzas that correspond to these paraphrases:
   a. Je marche sur l'avenue.
   b. Je suis très content.
   c. Je dis «bonjour.»
   d. Je parle à tout le monde.
   e. Tu vas rencontrer des amis.
   f. Tes amis sont amusants.
   g. Je vais au rendez-vous avec toi.

Types of Texts

Although both the song *Les Champs-Élysées* and the bus tour brochure describe things to see and do in and around Paris, they differ in several important ways.

1. Think about the different types of writing, then answer these questions.
   a. In what ways is the page layout of the song different from that of the bus tour brochure? Which one appeals to you more? Be prepared to tell why.
   b. Although one reading is from a brochure and the other is a song, in what ways are the two texts alike?

2. Review the purposes or goals of written work discussed on page 75, then answer these questions.
   a. For what purpose or purposes do you think the singer wrote this song?
   b. How are these purposes different from those of the brochure writer?
   c. In addition to their other goals, both writers probably wanted to illustrate the highlights and advantages of a city like Paris, although they chose to do it in different ways. What are the advantages and disadvantages of using a brochure format? a popular song?

3. Which kind of writing do you enjoy most—informative/explanatory writing like the brochure or poetic writing like the song? Be prepared to explain your choice.

NOTES CULTURELLES

In 50 B.C., Julius Caesar conquered the Gauls (the predecessors of the French) by defeating the last Gaul, Vercingétorix. According to the Astérix comics, one last village is able to hold out against the Romans. The villagers keep fighting the Romans because they have a magic potion that gives them superhuman strength. Astérix is the name of one of the cartoon warriors and a hero of many adventures. The Parc Astérix is an amusement park named in his honor. This theme park, located north of Paris, has several attractions, including a dolphin pool, rides, restaurants, and a lake.

PROJETS

1. Do some additional research on one of these topics:
   a. the design, history, and significance of your favorite building or monument in Paris (alternatively, select a building about which you know very little)
   b. Monet and his residence at Giverny—look into his life, the period during which he lived, his style, his paintings
   c. the history and design of Paris's most famous avenue, *les Champs-Élysées*
2. The song defines the *Champs-Élysées* as extending *de l'Étoile à la Concorde*. Find the two places on the map and pretend you are walking from one to the other. What other sites and buildings will you encounter? If you continue past *la Concorde*, what will you see? Where will you end up?
3. Write a poem about a monument in Paris.

This ad for the Parc Astérix shows Astérix and his best friend Obélix on one of the rides in the park.

À L'ORAL

Working with a partner, ask and answer the following question.

—*Tu veux aller aux Champs-Élysées?*
—*Oh, oui, j'aime ...*
    regarder les gens
    aller au café
    aller au cinéma
    faire une promenade
    visiter les monuments
    faire du shopping

PARC ASTÉRIX
une journée magique

LE FRANÇAIS EN AMÉRIQUE

If you had not looked at the chapter title, would you have known that these buildings are located in Canada? Where else might they have looked at home? The top building in the photograph is the Château Frontenac, now a luxury hotel. It also serves as the headquarters of the Canadian Pacific Railroad.

This site has played an important role in the history of Quebec City.

- Between 1620 and 1624, Samuel de Champlain built the Château Saint-Louis, the first important building in New France, near this site on the cliffs of the Saint Lawrence River.
- In 1784, the English governor Sir Frederick Haldimand built a new governor's residence behind the Château Saint-Louis, on the site of today's Château Frontenac.

Le français en Amérique du Nord

This reading tells the history of French-speaking people in North America. Before reading it, consider these questions.

1. Have you heard the word *francophone?*
   a. What does this word mean?
   b. What do you know about *la francophonie?*
2. You'll find out more about francophone cultures in this and the following chapters. First, test your knowledge by telling whether you think each of the following statements is *vrai* or *faux.*
   a. The word *francophone* refers to the French telephone system, which is one of the most advanced in the world.

b. French is spoken as a primary or official secondary language on five of the seven continents.
c. French is a primary or official secondary language in more than 40 countries around the world.
d. French is not spoken as a native language in any region of the United States.
e. French-speaking Canadians are concentrated in and around the city of Quebec, with few French speakers outside of that city.

Now read the passage and complete the activities that follow.

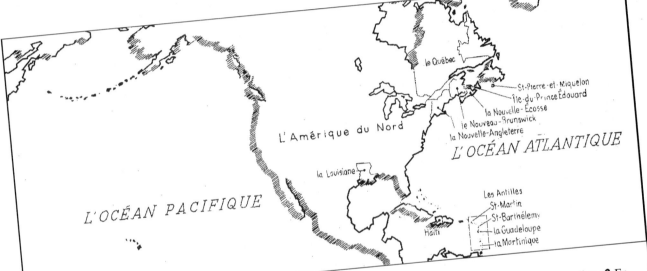

Quand est-ce que les Français sont venus dans le Nouveau Monde? La présence des Français dans le Nouveau Monde date depuis plus de 400 ans. En 1536 Jacques Cartier a commencé son exploration du Saint-Laurent. Les premiers colons français sont arrivés à peu près 50 ans plus tard. Ils ont navigué le Saint-Laurent et ont établi des villages sur les bords du grand fleuve.

Où est-ce que les colons français se sont établis dans le Nouveau Monde? En 1604, Samuel de Champlain est arrivé dans le Nouveau Monde accompagné d'autres colons. Ces colons ont occupé ce qui est aujourd'hui la Nouvelle-Écosse et une partie du Nouveau-Brunswick. Ils ont appelé cette région l'Acadie et ils se sont appelés Acadiens. Quatre ans plus tard, Samuel de Champlain a fondé la ville de Québec et il est devenu gouverneur de «la Nouvelle-France».

Qu'est-ce qui est arrivé aux Acadiens? En 1713 le Traité d'Utrecht a été signé. Ce traité a donné le pouvoir de gouverner le Nouveau Monde à l'Angleterre. Les Anglais ont demandé aux Acadiens de jurer leur fidélité à l'Angleterre. À peu près 6 000 Acadiens ont refusé de nier leur identité française. Alors, les Anglais ont envoyé ces colons français dans les colonies anglaises dans la Caroline du Sud; d'autres sont allés dans le Maine et puis en Louisiane. Là, le mot *Acadien* a été transformé au mot *Cajun.*

Est-ce qu'il y a encore des gens qui parlent français en Amérique du Nord? La présence française continue toujours dans l'Amérique du Nord. Il y a toujours des Américains qui parlent français comme langue maternelle, surtout dans le Maine et en Louisiane. En plus, on compte aujourd'hui plus de 7 millions de Canadiens d'origine française qui sont les descendants de colons. La plupart habitent dans la province du Québec.

ACTIVITÉ 1

1. Scan the passage, then select the two statements that reflect the main idea.
  a. French speakers in North America continue to affirm their identity in spite of over 200 years of living among English-speaking populations.
  b. We owe the presence of French-speaking populations in the United States to political struggles between the French and the English during the 18th century.
  c. Whether based on nationality, language, race, or beliefs, prejudice is unacceptable and results in much human unhappiness.

2. Several events in the history of Canada are mentioned in the reading passage. Correctly re-order these events by numbering them from 1 to 8.
  —Des colons arrivent dans le Nouveau-Brunswick et la Nouvelle Écosse.
  —Jacques Cartier commence ses explorations.
  —La France et l'Angleterre signent le Traité d'Utrecht.
  —Les colons qui parlent français sont persécutés par les Anglais.
  —Samuel de Champlain fonde la ville de Québec.
  —Les Acadiens sont déportés.
  —Samuel de Champlain devient gouverneur de la Nouvelle-France.
  —Les premiers colons français arrivent dans le Nouveau Monde.

3. In Chapter 11, we saw how important outlining is to understanding the structure and organization of a text. Outline the preceding passage. Then compare your outline with those of several classmates. Have you located the same main ideas and supporting details?

4. Ask a partner the headline questions in the reading passage. Have your partner answer the questions as briefly as possible, using the information contained in the paragraphs. Switch roles.

Point of View

In Chapter 13, we identified and analyzed differences in text types in terms of their style and purpose. Texts also differ in terms of their **point of view. Point of view** refers to the attitude the author takes toward the subject. For example:

- An author may be neutral, critical, or sympathetic toward one of the characters or groups in the passage.
- The author's approach to the material may be serious, critical, thoughtful, informal, or entertaining.

1. Is the author in sympathy with the French or the English in the passage? In other words, how do you think the author feels toward the English? toward the French?

2. How does the passage make you feel about the English? about the French?

3. Can the point of view change from one section of a work to another?

Mon pays

The next reading is a song well-known to French-speaking Canadians. Consider these questions before reading the lyrics of the song.

1. When you think of Canada, what images come to mind? Brainstorm for a few minutes to see how much you already know.

2. Do you associate a particular season with Canada? The Canadian singer Gilles Vigneault does. Quickly read over the first two lines of the song. Which season is it?

3. Now brainstorm again: What specific vocabulary words do you think Vigneault might use to describe this season?

Now read the song and do the activities that follow.

Au Canada, le Québec a produit de nombreux chanteurs de grand talent. Parmi eux, le chanteur-poète Gilles Vigneault. Dans *Mon pays* il exprime l'amour, l'amitié et son grand attachement à son pays. *Mon pays* est devenu très connu. On nomme parfois cette chanson *l'anthème national du Canadien français*.

Mon pays
—Gilles Vigneault—

1 Mon pays ce n'est pas un pays
2 c'est l'hiver
3 Mon jardin ce n'est pas un jardin
4 c'est la plaine
5 Mon chemin ce n'est pas un chemin
6 c'est la neige
7 Mon pays ce n'est pas un pays
8 c'est l'hiver

9 Dans la blanche cérémonie
10 où la neige au vent se marie
11 Dans ce pays de poudrerie
12 Mon père a fait bâtir maison
13 Et je m'en vais être fidèle
14 À sa manière à son modèle
15 La chambre d'ami sera telle
16 Qu'on viendra des autres saisons
17 Pour se bâtir à côté d'elle

18 Mon pays ce n'est pas un pays
19 c'est l'hiver
20 Mon refrain ce n'est pas un refrain
21 c'est rafale
22 Ma maison ce n'est pas ma maison

23 c'est froidure
24 Mon pays ce n'est pas un pays
25 c'est l'hiver

26 De mon grand pays solitaire
27 Je crie avant que de me taire
28 À tous les hommes de la Terre
29 Ma maison, c'est votre maison
30 Entre mes quatre murs de glace
31 Je mets mon temps et mon espace
32 À préparer le feu, la place
33 Pour les humains de l'horizon
34 Et les humains sont de ma race

[Refrain]

35 Mon pays ce n'est pas un pays
36 c'est l'envers
37 D'un pays qui n'était ni pays
38 Ni patrie
39 Ma chanson ce n'est pas ma chanson
40 c'est ma vie
41 c'est pour toi que je veux posséder
42 mes hivers

ACTIVITÉ 2

1. Scan the passage, then tell which statements best describe the song.
   a. This song tells the history of French-speaking people in Canada.
   b. The song is about the weather in French-speaking Canada.
   c. The song is a message of welcome to all people from the French in Canada.

2. Reread the first refrain (lines 1–8) and list all of the words that describe the weather.

3. Read the first stanza (lines 9–17).
   a. The wintery description is continued in the first three lines. Describe in your own words what the living conditions must be like in a place where winter is such a dominant theme.
   b. In spite of the weather, what did the singer's father decide to do? Do you think that the singer approves of his father's choice of a place to live?
   c. What do you think this stanza says about the heartiness of the French Canadian? about French Canadian friendship and hospitality?

4. The second stanza (lines 2–34) is an invitation.
   a. Who does the inviting? Who is invited?
   b. To what or where are they invited? What do the *quatre murs de glace* in line 30 represent?

   c. What does this stanza say about the French Canadian response to others, about individual differences, and about respect for humankind?

5. Summarize the last stanza (lines 35–42). What message is the artist trying to convey?

6. Write a poem about the place where you live. Follow this "formula" or another of your choice.
   Line 1: State the city or region name.
   Lines 2-3: Name three physical/geographical features or important cities, then list three adjectives that describe them.
   Lines 4-5: Write two adjectives that describe its weather, and state in one or two words your feelings about the weather.
   Lines 6-8: Write three short sentences that describe popular activities or pastimes.
   Line 9: Write two adjectives that describe these activities.
   Line 10: Write your overall evaluation of your city.

> **BONUS:** Why might this song sometimes be called the French Canadian National Anthem?

Types of Texts

1. In the previous chapter, we looked at passages in this reader to find examples of several different types of texts. In what ways is this text similar to and different from those we have read to this point?

2. We have noted that authors select different text types to convey their messages. Although this text is clearly a song, it has characteristics of other text types, too. In what ways might it be considered:
   a. a poem?
   b. an advertisement or publicity statement?
   c. a declaration or an explanation?

3. In Chapter 13, we listed and analyzed many different purposes of writing. What do you think was the author's purpose in writing this song?

4. Earlier in this chapter, we focused on the point of view of a written work. Quickly review the definition of **point of view.**
   a. What is the author's attitude toward the wintery weather, the people of Canada, and the values of the people of Canada?
   b. What do you think is the author's point of view in this song?

NOTES CULTURELLES

Le Québec libre

The French Canadian separatist movement uses as its slogan *Vive le Québec libre*. The movement's goals are to establish the province of Quebec as a sovereign state, separate from Canada. The new Quebec would represent the French culture and language in North America.

French Canadian singers

There are many French Canadian singers—among them, Robert Charlebois, Félix Leclerc, Fabienne Thibault, Pauline Julien, Diane Dufresne. Most of them sing about their French identity and also about their identity as Canadians.

À L'ORAL

Work with a partner to find out his or her preferences in music. Exchange roles.

—*Tu aimes...*
  la musique classique?
  le rock?
  le reggae?
  la musique populaire?
  la musique folklorique?
—*Oui, j'aime...*
or
—*Non, je n'aime pas...*
or
—*Je préfère...*

PROJETS

1. Similes (pronounced *si-mi-lees*) and metaphors (pronounced *me-ta-fors*) are literary comparisons in which one person or thing is described in terms of another. For example, you might say *"My younger brother is a monster,"* or *"My best friend is just like a guardian angel."*
   * A simile is a comparison that uses *like* or *as*.
     The winter wind is as sharp as a knife.
     Le vent d'hiver est tranchant comme un couteau.
     The winter wind is like a knife.
     Le vent d'hiver est comme un couteau.
   * A metaphor is a comparison in which something is said to be something else.
     The winter wind is a wolf that scratches at my door.
     Le vent d'hiver est un loup qui gratte à ma porte.
   There are many literary comparisons in *Mon pays*. Find them. Does Gilles Vigneault use similes, metaphors, or both? Use a simile or a metaphor to describe where you live.
2. We have learned from the reading that French is spoken as a native language in parts of New England and Louisiana. Can you identify other populations in other regions of the United States for whom English is not the primary language? Are there ethnic groups whose heritage, customs, and possibly language are particular to your city or part of the country?

CHAPITRE 15

LE FRANÇAIS EN AFRIQUE

The photograph illustrates a street scene in Dakar, the capital of Senegal, a French-speaking country. How would you know that the photograph was taken in a French-speaking area? Look at the photograph and see if you can find any indications. Then read the following short description of Senegal and find the country on a map.

Le Sénégal est un pays de l'Afrique de l'ouest. Le Sénégal est situé au sud de la Mauritanie et au nord de la Guinée. C'est un territoire qui a plus de 196 000 km² et plus de 7 millions d'habitants. Le Sénégal est une ancienne colonie française qui a déclaré son indépendance en 1960. La langue officielle du Sénégal est le français, mais plus de 80% de la population parle le wolof, une langue africaine.

Le français en Afrique

Before reading this article, test your knowledge about Africa by telling whether the following statements are *vrai* or *faux*.

1. Africa is a continent in which the only language spoken is English.
2. A substantial number of people in Africa speak French.
3. French is spoken only in Europe.
4. There are many famous French writers of African descent.
5. In addition to French, people in Africa speak African languages.

Now read the article and complete the activities that follow.

LA FRANCOPHONIE

Plus de 100 millions de gens parlent le français dans le monde. Le français est considéré aujourd'hui comme langue universelle. Elle exprime les différences ethniques de plusieurs peuples dans le monde entier. On trouve des francophones dans les régions suivantes: en Europe, en Afrique, en Amérique, en Asie et en Océanie.

LE FRANÇAIS EN AFRIQUE

C'est au 19e siècle, pendant la IIIe République que la France a fondé un grand empire colonial. Cet empire s'étendait partout dans le monde, mais était centré sur l'Afrique du Nord et sur l'Afrique Noire. Avant la Deuxième Guerre Mondiale, la France était la seconde puissance coloniale dans le monde. Mais après la guerre, en moins de vingt ans, l'empire colonial a cessé d'exister. La colonisation a éveillé chez les peuples dominés l'aspiration de la liberté.

La langue française est la langue principale (ou officielle) ou bien une langue parlée par une grande partie de la population de l'Afrique. En Afrique du Nord, le Maroc, l'Algérie et la Tunisie sont des pays où beaucoup de gens parlent encore le français. En Afrique Occidentale (de l'Ouest), un grand nombre de pays ont adopté le français comme langue officielle: la Mauritanie, le Mali, le Niger, le Tchad, le Sénégal, la Guinée, la Côte-d'Ivoire, le Burkina Faso, le Togo, le Bénin, le Cameroun, le Gabon, le Congo, le Zaïre et la République Centrafricaine. On parle aussi français en la République Malgache et dans les Îles Comores.

ÉCRIVAINS CÉLÈBRES

Plusieurs écrivains de langue française sont devenus célèbres. Originaire de la Martinique,

Aimé Césaire est un des plus connus. Son recueil de poèmes *Cahier d'un retour au pays natal*, publié en 1939, a eu un très grand succès. **Léopold Senghor**, originaire du Sénégal, homme de lettres et aussi premier président du Sénégal, a été élu membre de l'Académie française en 1983. À ces noms il faut ajouter, parmi d'autres, celui de **Léon Damas,** poète guyanais, et de **Camara Laye,** écrivain de Haute Guinée.

ACTIVITÉ 1

1. Scan the passage and then tell which statements most appropriately summarize the main idea.
   a. French is spoken only in some areas of Europe, especially in France and in Belgium.
   b. French is an international language and is spoken widely throughout the world.
   c. A large number of countries in Western Africa use French as their official language.
   d. Many famous African writers have chosen French as their language.
   e. Most of the African writers who write in French have achieved only local fame.

2. Select those countries in which French is either the principal language, the official language, or is spoken by a large percentage of the population.
   a. l'Afrique du Sud   e. le Togo
   b. le Niger   f. le Zaïre
   c. la Libye   g. le Mali
   d. le Soudan   h. le Yémen

3. Match the African writers with their country of origin.
   a. le Sénégal   ___ Aimé Césaire
   b. la Guyane   ___ Léopold Senghor
   c. la Martinique   ___ Léon Damas
   d. la Haute Guinée   ___ Camara Laye

4. With a partner, use the map of Africa to locate the various countries. Follow the model and switch roles.
   —Où se trouve...
      le Zaïre   le Cameroun
      le Sénégal   l'Algérie
      le Maroc   le Tchad?
   —Le Sénégal se trouve... de l'Afrique.
      dans le nord
      à l'ouest
      à l'est
      au centre
      dans le sud

Guessing the Meaning from Context

Many students of foreign languages believe that to read a passage means to translate each word from the foreign language into English. Many have also adopted the habit of actually writing in the English in small letters between the lines of text. This habit does not lead to progress in reading. The reason is simple: looking up each word wastes time and does not take advantage of the meaning that can be derived from the context.

For example, consider the English sentence, "That summer there was a dearth of clams; they couldn't be found at any price." If you read the sentence, stopped at the first hard word, "dearth," and looked it up in the dictionary, you would be wasting your time. The context provides the meaning. You only have to read on without stopping until you reach the end of the sentence or paragraph. Can you guess what "dearth" means without looking it up? Do the words "they couldn't be found at any price" help you determine its meaning?

You can use the same process in French. Read the following sentences:

Mais, après la guerre, en moins de vingt ans, l'empire colonial a cessé d'exister. La colonisation a éveillé chez les peuples dominés l'aspiration de la liberté.

If the colonial empire ceased to exist, what could have happened? Can you guess the meaning of the words *a éveillé* from the context?

L'homme qui te ressemble

Often when we think of people from other countries or of other races, the differences are what we stress. They are the things we see and feel first. The following poem takes another point of view: it tells about the similarities between peoples. Before reading it, consider these questions.

1. Think about the things that make people the same rather than different.

2. What basic needs are the same for all people in the world? Make a list.

Now read the poem and do the activities that follow.

L'homme qui te ressemble—
René Philombe, poète camerounais.

1 J'ai frappé à ta porte
2 j'ai frappé à ton cœur
3 pour avoir bon lit
4 pour avoir bon feu
5 pourquoi me repousser?
6 Ouvre-moi mon frère!...

7 Pourquoi me demander
8 si je suis d'Afrique
9 si je suis d'Amérique
10 si je suis d'Asie
11 si je suis d'Europe?
12 Ouvre-moi mon frère!...

13 Pourquoi me demander
14 la longueur de mon nez
15 l'épaisseur de ma
   bouche
16 la couleur de ma peau
17 et le nom de mes dieux?
18 Ouvre-moi mon frère!...

19 Je ne suis pas un noir
20 je ne suis pas un rouge
21 je ne suis pas un jaune
22 je ne suis pas un blanc
23 mais je ne suis qu'un
   homme
24 Ouvre-moi mon frère!...

25 Ouvre-moi ta porte
26 Ouvre-moi ton cœur
27 car je suis un homme
28 l'homme de tous les
   temps
29 l'homme de tous les
   cieux
30 l'homme qui te
   ressemble!...

ACTIVITÉ 2

1. Scan the poem, then select the statements that most appropriately reflect the main idea.
   a. The poem emphasizes the differences among people.
   b. Philombe is trying to say that all people have the same needs and feelings.
   c. Physical differences are very important, according to the poem.
   d. The poem expresses the universality of humankind.
2. In the first stanza:
   a. Where has the poet knocked?
   b. What has he asked for?
   c. What does he want opened?
   d. He says that people have the same basic goals. What are they?
3. In the second stanza, name the continents he may be from.
4. In the third stanza, is he describing geographical location or physical features? Which ones?
5. In the fourth stanza:
   a. What kinds of peoples does he refer to?
   b. Write in one sentence the main idea of this stanza.
   c. The poet expresses the differences that are usually perceived among people. What are they?
6. In the last stanza the poet gives four reasons why the reader should not be influenced by appearances or differences in beliefs. What are they?
7. What is the overall message of this poem? What ideas is the poet trying to convey? How do you feel about the message?

> **BONUS:** Look up Cameroon in an encyclopedia. Find three interesting facts about the country to share with your classmates.

Guessing the Meaning from Context

In reading the poem by René Philombe, you no doubt came across several words that you did not actually understand but could guess from the context. For instance, in the first stanza, the poet asks to be let into a house to get some comfort. He says *pour avoir bon lit / pour avoir bon feu*. If you know that the poet wants some comfort, can you guess what *bon lit* and *bon feu* might mean?

In the third stanza, the poet wonders why people put so much importance on the features of the face. Can you now guess what the phrases *la longueur de mon nez / l'épaisseur de ma bouche / la couleur de ma peau* might mean?

NOTES CULTURELLES

Le colonialisme

During the 19th century, several countries, including Great Britain and France, undertook the colonization of Africa, Asia, and other parts of the world. France established colonies in most of West Africa, and made the people living there dependent on it.

Le Cameroun

The poet René Philombe is from the African country of Cameroon. Cameroon is a West African nation bordered by Nigeria, Chad, the Central African Republic, the Congo, Equatorial Guinea, and Gabon. After World War I, France became the trustee of 80 percent of the area, while the British became trustee of 20 percent. In 1960 Cameroon became independent. People native to Cameroon are likely to speak French and English in addition to their native African language.

À L'ORAL

Imagine that you are meeting a person from another country for the first time. What would you say to begin a conversation? The following might be a good way to start:

—*Comment t'appelles-tu?*
—*Je m'appelle...*
—*Où habites-tu?*
—*J'habite à...*(town).

Work with a partner and list two or three more questions you would ask. Practice asking and answering these questions.

PROJETS

1. Look back at the first reading passage in this chapter. Several countries were mentioned, including Senegal, Mali, the Ivory Coast, etc. Look up these countries in an encyclopedia to find out more about them. Who are the people that inhabit these countries? What kind of government do they have? What are their principal products? What other languages do the people speak?

2. Several famous writers in addition to René Philombe are mentioned in this chapter. Who are they? Choose one and try to find out more about him. Information will probably be easier to locate for writers such as Senghor and Césaire than for Philombe. Prepare a short report to present to the class.

3. Using *L'homme qui te ressemble* as a model, write a poem about the similarities between Americans.

C H A P I T R E 16
QU'EST-CE QU'ON VA MANGER?

1. Which of the following stores are shown in the photographs?
   une boucherie   *une pâtisserie*   *une charcuterie*
2. How many of the products shown can you name in French?
3. In which of the three stores listed above would the following items be found?

une tartelette	*un bifteck*	*une baguette*
un saucisson	*du canard*	*une pâtisserie*
du pain	*des croissants*	*une salade de tomates*
un poulet	*un rôti*	*une salade composée*
un éclair	*du jambon*	*un gâteau au chocolat*

- Are there small specialty food stores comparable to these where you live? If so, does your family shop there often or only on occasion? Why?

Les plats cuisinés

When one thinks of France, one often thinks immediately of wonderful food. But what about shopping in France? It's a snap! The French shop in immense, all-purpose stores called *hypermarchés*, in somewhat smaller *supermarchés*, and in small specialty stores.

Before reading these fliers, answer the following questions.

1. In what types of foods do the following small stores specialize? What is the difference between the stores in each pair?
   a. une boulangerie, une pâtisserie
   b. une boucherie, une charcuterie

2. Did you know that in France there are:
   8,724 boulangeries
   27,523 boulangeries/pâtisseries
   32,906 boucheries
   10,813 charcuteries

Reread these statistics and try to explain why:
   a. there are so many *boulangeries/pâtisseries*
   b. there are so many more *boucheries* than *charcuteries*

Now read the advertisements and do the activities that follow.

ACTIVITÉ 1

1. Scan the advertisements, then choose the best summary.
   a. A variety of meats and prepared meat dishes are offered in the advertisements.
   b. Meats and prepared meat dishes are available in both *la boucherie* and *la charcuterie.*
   c. Based on these advertisements, it appears that while a *boucherie* usually does not carry pork products, a *charcuterie* may carry beef, lamb, and poultry products in addition to pork.

2. Reread the *boucherie* ad to find out the following information.
   a. Which types of meat are offered?
   —veal —turkey —chicken —rabbit
   —pork —beef —seafood —lamb
   b. Which type of meat is most frequently advertised?
   c. In what unit of measure (pounds, grams, kilograms, etc.) is meat sold?
   d. Which is the least expensive meat?
   e. Is beef always more expensive than any other meat?
   f. Given this selection, which meat(s) would you order?

3. Reread the *charcuterie* advertisement to locate these details:
   a. Does this section of the *charcuterie* advertisement offer meat or deli items?
   b. Look for the large headings. What kinds

of meats can be purchased that are prepared in advance?
   c. Which dishes are the most expensive? Can you explain why?
   d. Which of the individual meals would you prefer? Be prepared to tell why you are not interested in the other choices.

> **BONUS:** Look at the prices. In what monetary unit are they expressed? What is different about the way prices are written in France and the United States?

4. Using the *boucherie* and *charcuterie* advertisements, practice ordering both the meat item and the deli item you selected in questions 2 and 3 above.
   —*Je voudrais ___ kilos de ___, s'il vous plaît. Vous en avez?*
   —*Vous voulez bien ___ kilos de ___?*
   —*C'est ça.*
   or
   —*Non. Je désire ___ kilos de ___.*
   —*Ah, bon.*

5. Based on what you have learned about the number of small stores in France and the types of foods they sell, what do you think are the advantages of such a manner of shopping?

Dictionary Skills

In any language, many words have several meanings.
• Think about the English word *bark*. How many different meanings can you list?
• With a partner or in a small group, brainstorm for a few minutes about the word *cross*. This word has even more meanings.

Native speakers of a language select the appropriate meaning of a word in a particular sentence by relating the word and its definition to the subject of the conversation. In other words, they rely on context.
   When looking up words in a dictionary, remember that terms often have several meanings and that we must select the appropriate one for the context.
• Look up the French words *prendre* and *marché*. How many different meanings are there? In what contexts are they used?

La cuisine

When you go to a French *charcuterie,* you can buy the main ingredients for a hot sandwich as well as some prepared dishes. The following are two recipes for quick and easy meals. The first recipe is for a well-known French ham and cheese sandwich called a *croque-monsieur;* the main ingredients can be bought in the *charcuterie.* The second is for a type of salad made in Nice; you can buy this salad already prepared in the *charcuterie.*

Before reading the recipes, make two lists.

1. List the ingredients that you would expect to find in a sandwich or a fancy salad. List as many ingredients as you can in French.
2. List the terms you might encounter when reading a recipe, including units of weight and measure, names of utensils, and basic actions like measuring and stirring.

Now read the recipes and do the activities that follow.

Croque-Monsieur (1 pers)

ALLUMEZ LE FOUR (7) *

COUPEZ 2 TRANCHES DE PAIN DE MIE.
ENLEVEZ LES BORDS.
COUPEZ 1 TRANCHE DE JAMBON BLANC
A LA MÊME TAILLE QUE LE PAIN.
BEURREZ CHAQUE TRANCHE DE PAIN
AVEC 1 *cuillère à café* DE BEURRE.
DÉCOUPEZ 12 LAMELLES DE GRUYÈRE.
SUR LA TRANCHE
DE PAIN DE MIE BEURRÉE
POSEZ 6 LAMELLES DE GRUYÈRE
PUIS LA TRANCHE DE JAMBON
PUIS 6 LAMELLES DE GRUYÈRE
PUIS LA 2ᵉ TRANCHE DE PAIN DE MIE.
(coté beurré vers le gruyère)
METTEZ LE CROQUE-MONSIEUR
AU FOUR *sur la grille*
10 MINUTES.
RETOURNEZ-LE.
ENCORE AU FOUR
3 MINUTES.

Mangez chaud.

*7 = 350° F

Salade Niçoise (2 pers)

COUVREZ LE FOND DU PLAT
AVEC DES FEUILLES DE LAITUE (6 environ)
COUPEZ 4 TOMATES LAVEES *en tranches.*
COUVREZ-EN LES FEUILLES DE LAITUE.
COUPEZ 1/2 POIVRON VERT *en fines lamelles.*
ET 1/2 PETIT OIGNON.
COUVREZ-EN LES TOMATES.
COUPEZ 1 ŒUF DUR *en 8 rondelles.*
POSEZ *les rondelles* SUR LES POIVRONS.
OUVREZ UNE *petite* BOITE D'ANCHOIS
POSEZ-LES SUR *les rondelles* D'ŒUF.
METTEZ SUR LA SALADE
6 OLIVES VERTES ET
6 OLIVES NOIRES.

VINAIGRETTE.
METTEZ DANS UN PETIT BOL
1 *cuillère à soupe* DE VINAIGRE
1/2 *cuillère à café* DE MOUTARDE
ET 4 *pincées* DE SEL.
AJOUTEZ
3 *cuillères à soupe* D'HUILE.
MELANGEZ

ACTIVITÉ 2

1. Skim the recipes, then choose the statement that most closely summarizes them.
   a. After preparing the ingredients, mixing, and measuring, both dishes must be cooked.
   b. The sandwich and the salad seem quite similar to dishes available in an American deli or carry-out section of a supermarket.
   c. Both recipes are long and complicated.

2. Read the recipe for the sandwich.
   a. What is the first thing you need to do?
   b. Skim the recipe to find the units of measure. How is the term "teaspoon" expressed?
   c. Find and list the action verbs that tell you what to do.
   d. Reread the recipe; look specifically for cooking instructions. How is the sandwich to be served?
   e. Reread the recipe and write out a grocery list for the items you will need to make the sandwich.

3. Read the recipe for the salad.
   a. Skim the recipe to find the units of measure. How is the term "tablespoon" expressed? How is salt measured in this recipe?
   b. Find and list the action verbs that tell you what to do. Which actions are the same in both recipes?
   c. What decorative touches make the salad more attractive?
   d. Reread the recipe and write out a grocery list for the ingredients in the salad and the salad dressing.

BONUS:
- In American recipes, oven temperatures are indicated in degrees Fahrenheit. How is the oven temperature indicated in the sandwich recipe? How hot do you think this probably is?
- How many people does the salad serve?

Dictionary Skills

Earlier in this chapter, we brainstormed about the many different meanings for the words *bark* and *cross*. Each different meaning:
- may represent a different part of speech (a noun, a verb, an adjective, or an adverb)
- probably corresponds to a completely different word in another language.

Read the following sentences and tell which part of speech (noun, verb, adjective, adverb) each word in italics represents.
1. My dog *barks* whenever a stranger comes into the yard.
2. The *bark* on that tree is uneven and covered with pitch.
3. I have to *cross* that street to get to the supermarket.
4. Poisons are marked with a skull and *crossbones*.
5. *Cross* it off the grocery list once you have put it in the basket.
6. The butcher was really *cross* today.

Now look at the recipes in French. The word *mettre* is used several times. Look up the word and pay particular attention to its many different meanings. The verb *to beat* is frequently used in recipes. Look up this word in the English-to-French part of your dictionary. How many different meanings (both nouns and verbs) are offered for the word *beat*? Which French word is appropriate in a recipe?

NOTES CULTURELLES

Here are several tips on what to do while shopping in France.

1. Bring a sturdy shopping bag in which to carry your purchases. Small stores generally do not provide bags for you. Some people like to use *un filet* to carry their purchases home. This small net bag is easy to carry in a purse or backpack and expands to hold many things.

2. At the supermarket you are expected to bag your own groceries. Plastic bags may be provided for you, but you'll have to put your purchases in them.

3. At the supermarket, do not handle the fruits and vegetables. Grocers generally prohibit squeezing and poking because it damages the produce. They will be glad to take your order and will select the items you desire.

PROJETS

1. Get together in small groups to prepare the foods described in the recipes. Bring the ingredients for either the *salade niçoise* or the *croque-monsieur* and make them for your class.
2. Using the vocabulary from the two recipes, write in French a simple recipe for one of your favorite salads or sandwiches.

À L'ORAL

1. With a partner, role-play a scene that might take place at the *charcuterie* or at the market. The following general guidelines may be helpful.
   a. Greet the storekeeper.
   b. Inquire about what items are available.
      —*Vous avez de la salade niçoise aujourd'hui?*
      —*Oui...*
   c. Request the price.
      —*Combien coûte la salade niçoise?*
      —*La salade coûte...*
   d. Say good-bye.

2. Play the role of chef and demonstrate how to prepare one of the recipes in this chapter or another item of your choice that could be found in a *charcuterie*. Be sure to name your ingredients and to describe your actions as you prepare the food.

CHAPITRE 17

A^U SUPERMARCHÉ

1. In which of the following stores might these photographs have been taken?

    une boucherie   *une boulangerie*   *un marché en plein air*
    une charcuterie   *une épicerie*   *un supermarché*

2. Indicate which fruits and vegetables are shown in the photographs.

    —*Il y a des...*
    —*Il n'y a pas de (d')...*

    tomates   *poivrons verts*   *bananes*
    avocats   *champignons*   *oranges*
    concombres   *choux-fleur*   *choux*
    pommes

Les produits alimentaires

Fruits and vegetables are wonderful when eaten fresh, but are also healthy when included in prepared and canned foods. These labels for a variety of food items were collected in Canada, where food products must be labeled in both English and French.

1. Can you explain why bilingual labeling is required?

2. To what extent do you think that this is a good idea?

3. Make a list of the types of information you would expect to find on a canned food product label.

Now read the labels and do the activities that follow.

ACTIVITÉ 1

1. Scan the labels, then choose the statements that best summarize them. Correct any statements that are false.
   a. Labels for food products always include the ingredients, in decreasing order of their volume in the product.
   b. Labels may include the ingredients but must indicate the weight or amount of each ingredient listed.
   c. Labels for food products must include the ingredients and the directions for use of the product.
2. Look quickly over the food labels. Which items are to be served hot? cold? hot or cold?
3. Which food item(s):
   a. is (are) made with fresh milk?
   b. include(s) salt? sugar? vegetable oil?
   c. contain(s) nothing artificial?

4. Reread the labels and answer these questions.
   a. Which vegetables in the soup do you like? Which don't you care for?
   b. How much tea mix should you add per glass? per pitcher?
   c. Is real butter used to flavor the popcorn?
   d. How many times is the expression *lait frais* repeated in the pudding label? Why do you think this is true?
5. Discuss the ingredients found in the various foods with a partner. Ask and answer the following question. Exchange roles.
   —*Qu'est-ce qu'il y a dans le potage?*
   —*Il y a des carottes, des pois....*
   —*Qu'est-ce qu'il y a dans le pouding Nestlé?*
   —*Il y a du...*

Dictionary Skills—English to French

We have seen that although two words may be spelled in the same way, their meanings may be very different. They may even be different parts of speech. Notice the abbreviations the dictionary uses for parts of speech:
noun—*n.*   verb—*v.*   adjective—*adj.*   adverb—*adv.*

Here is a typical English-to-French dictionary entry for the word **bark**.
   bark n.f. écorce (botanique); n.m. aboiement; v. aboyer

1. Which word(s) is (are) nouns? verbs?
2. Can you tell which word you would use to tell what a dog does?
3. Which of the two nouns corresponds to the outer covering of a tree? What hint helped you to answer this question?

Here is the dictionary entry for the word **cross**.
   cross n.f. croix; n.m. croisement (de route); adj. contraire, opposé, désagréable; v. croiser, traverser; v. contrarier; *to cross out*, barrer; *crossword*, mots croisés; *river crossing*, gué; *railroad crossing*, passage à niveau; *sea crossing*, traversée

1. How are the different parts of speech indicated?
2. What word would you use in the following situations? You may need to use your dictionary.
   a crossing in a road   to make someone mad
   a journey across the ocean   to cross the park
   a cross old man   to cross something out
   an X on a questionnaire
3. Is the gender of the French translation always provided? What gender is the word *croix*? What gender is the word *gué*? How can you find out?
4. When looking up a word, how can you be sure that the translation you select really corresponds to the meaning you want?

À l'Intermarché

Where do you and your family shop when you need:

- just a few snack items?
- enough groceries to make a birthday dinner for a parent or best friend?
- groceries, small hardware items, and oil for the family car?

In France, there are also different sizes and types of stores. Did you know that in France there are:

- 580 hypermarchés
- 5 917 supermarchés
- 5 888 supérettes

Read over the following information about these three types of stores, and decide to which group the INTERMARCHÉ, advertised below, belongs. Then do the activities that follow.

LA SUPÉRETTE

C'est un petit libre-service qui joue le rôle d'un magasin de proximité en ville ou dans les villages. Les supérettes offrent un assortiment réduit de produits alimentaires ainsi qu'une gamme de produits non alimentaires d'achats fréquents (droguerie, entretien, hygiène, etc).

LES SUPERMARCHÉS

Le premier supermarché a fait son apparition en France en 1958. Les supermarchés sont des établissements indépendants qui vendent l'ensemble des produits alimentaires et qui offrent un assortiment plus ou moins important de produits non-alimentaires. Dans un supermarché, la vente s'y fait en libre-service. On paie à des postes de paiement à la sortie.

LES HYPERMARCHÉS

Le premier magasin de ce type est apparu en France en 1963, à Sainte-Geneviève-des-Bois, dans la région parisienne. Il portait l'enseigne de «Carrefour». Les hypermarchés sont des magasins:

- qui sont localisés à la périphérie des grandes villes
- qui sont facilement accessibles
- qui sont disposés d'un grand parking
- qui offrent en plus du magasin de nombreux services: des cafétérias, des centres auto, des centres d'équipement du foyer, des centres jardiniers, etc.
- qui fonctionnent en libre-service avec une ligne de caisses à la sortie
- qui pratiquent une politique de marges et des prix réduits

INTERMARCHE
Les Mousquetaires de la Distribution

LE CHOIX

INTERMARCHÉ est orienté vers les produits alimentaires mais vous allez trouver le textile, le petit matériel de cuisine, d'électro-ménager, d'électricité, etc.

LA QUALITE

Nous, on est des professionnels de l'alimentation. Toute une équipe de spécialistes va s'attacher à vous le prouver. Chaque responsable de rayon vous attend tous les jours dans votre **INTERMARCHÉ** pour vous guider dans vos achats. Faites-leur confiance. Ils connaissent leur métier.

LA FRAICHEUR

INTERMARCHÉ s'engage à vous garantir la fraîcheur! Vous allez trouver les produits de qualité tous les jours dans votre **INTERMARCHÉ.**

ACTIVITÉ 2

1. Skim the three paragraphs and accompanying advertisement, then tell whether the following statements are *vrai* or *faux*.

  a. The three types of stores described in the passage do not differ significantly from their counterparts in the United States.

  b. Based on the description of a *supérette*, such stores are not available here.

  c. The *hypermarché* seems to provide the broadest range of products and services.

2. Indicate which kind of store(s) each statement describes.

  a. Il n'y a pas de postes de paiement ni de lignes de caisses.

  b. C'est un libre-service.

  c. Les prix sont les plus bas.

  d. On peut y acheter quelque chose pour le jardin.

  e. On y offre des produits alimentaires et non-alimentaires.

  f. Le choix d'achat est limité aux produits les plus communs.

  g. Ils se trouvent dans tous les quartiers.

  h. On les trouve seulement à la périphérie des grandes villes.

  i. Pas trop grand et pas trop petit, on y offre un assortiment intéressant de produits.

  j. On peut y aller pour faire ses courses et pour faire réparer sa voiture.

  k. C'est le plus petit des magasins.

3. Reread the advertisement for the INTER-MARCHÉ.

  a. To which of the three categories of stores do you think it belongs? Be prepared to explain your choice.

  b. What three major sales points does this advertisement stress?

4. How does the INTERMARCHÉ advertisement respond to people who claim:

  a. that such stores have poor-quality produce?

  b. that such stores do not provide qualified and knowledgeable staff?

  c. that in such stores, the personal relationship between salesperson and shopper is destroyed?

BONUS: Do you find this advertisement convincing? Why or why not?

Dictionary Skills—French to English

Words and expressions never correspond directly from one language to another.

1. Take, for example, the English word *get*. Make a list of all of the expressions you can think of that use *get*:

  a. to get up

  b. to get off

  c. to get down

  d. to get ready

  e. ....

Use a dictionary to find the French verbs that correspond to each of these expressions.

2. In French, the verb *prendre* has several different meanings and is used in a variety of expressions. Look up this word in the French side of your dictionary and list all of the different meanings. How many are there? Use as many as you can in a sentence.

NOTES CULTURELLES

The following statistics provide details about annual French consumption of cheeses and escargots. Do you think the statistics would be the same in your state?

- **40 000 tonnes d'escargots**
- **1 202 000 tonnes de fromages**

gruyère	38 068 tonnes
roquefort	14 720 tonnes
cantal	19 039 tonnes
camembert	6 724 tonnes

À L'ORAL

Here is a list of several different kinds of prepared foods. Find out your classmate's preferences. Ask and answer the question according to the model.

—*Tu aimes le potage végétarien?*
—*Moi, je préfère la soupe aux tomates.*

> le potage végétarien
> le potage au poulet
> la soupe aux tomates
>
> le thé nature
> le thé au citron
> le thé à la menthe
>
> le pouding au tapioca
> le pouding à la vanille
> le pouding au chocolat

PROJETS

1. The INTERMARCHÉ advertisement claimed certain advantages for their supermarket. Write a similar advertisement to describe the advantages of a small *supérette*. What would you call your store?
2. Make a label in French for a canned or packaged food product of your choice. Be sure to include weights, ingredients, and directions for use.
3. As a class, make a collage of advertisements for food products.

CHAPITRE 18

ALLONS À LA SAMARITAINE!

Look at the picture of the department store. Note the large letters on the roof. Several things about the building are interesting.

1. How would you describe the style of the building? Is it a modern store? Is it a store that is likely to have been in business for many years?

2. In North America, large department stores are usually located in shopping malls. Where do you think this store is located? Compare it to a store in your town.

À la Samaritaine

The following selections from *la Samaritaine* brochure describe services that are available at the department store. Before reading them, answer the following questions.

1. What kinds of information do you expect to be provided?

2. Aside from sales, what additional services may be provided by a department store? Make a list.

Now read the brochure and do the activities that follow.

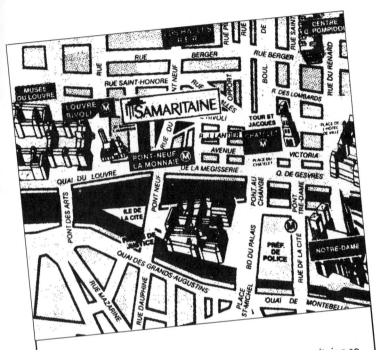

■ En plein cœur de Paris, face au Pont-Neuf, la Samaritaine se situe à proximité du Musée du Louvre, de Notre-Dame de Paris et de Beaubourg, Centre Georges Pompidou.

⫞SAMARITAINE

- ■ 19, rue de la Monnaie 75001 Paris
- ■ Télèphone: (1) 40.41.20.20
- ■ Métro Rer : Pont-Neuf, Châtelet Les Halles, Louvre.
- ■ Bus: lignes 21, 24, 27, 38, 47, 58, 67, 69, 70, 74, 75, 76, 81, 85 et 96
- ■ Magasins ouverts: lundi, mardi, mercredi, vendredi, samedi, 9h30 - 19h00, jeudi 9h30 - 22h.

Services

■ Pour vous être agréable, la Samaritaine vous propose des services qui vous faciliteront votre séjour à Paris:
- ● Bureau de change. Mag. 2 - Rez-de-chaussée.
- ● Bureau de détaxe. Mag. 2 - Sous-sol.
- ● Deux restaurants, le Grill et le Self-Service avec la vue sur la Seine. Mag. 2 - 5e étage.

■ Et pour votre plaisir:
- ● La terrasse avec restaurant en été, la plus belle vue de Paris, sur les bords de la Seine.
- ● La table d'orientation, Paris sur 360°.

ACTIVITÉ 1

1. Reread the list of services provided by *la Samaritaine*, then tell which statement most accurately summarizes them.
   a. *La Samaritaine* provides a complete range of services for the shopper and the tourist.
   b. Although it is a major department store, it is a little out of the way and not very easily accessible.
   c. *La Samaritaine* provides extra services to its clientele.
2. Look at the map and locate the metro stations near *la Samaritaine*. How many do you find? Is the department store conveniently located? In which part of Paris is it located? Near what famous Paris landmark can you find the store?
3. How many bus lines can you use to get to the store?
4. When is it open? What are the hours?
5. Now look at the list of extra services that the store provides. What services are listed? In what store are they located?
6. What service is available for the shopper's pleasure? What are its features?

BONUS: On what floors are the special services located? To what floor numbers do they correspond in an American building?

7. Suppose you are at *la Samaritaine* department store and then wanted to go to the Louvre. Would it be far? Could you get there on foot? Look at the map and tell how you would get there.
8. Tell a partner how you would get to the Notre-Dame cathedral from *la Samaritaine*. Use some of the following expressions.
   —*Allez tout droit.*
   —*Tournez à...*
      droite   gauche.
   —*Prenez...*
      le boulevard le quai
      le pont   l'avenue
   —*Traversez...*
      la rue   le pont
      l'avenue   le boulevard

Dictionary Skills

We have seen that words may have several different meanings and that these meanings vary according to context. For instance, the French word *vue* can be either a noun or a verb form. Find the word in the *Services* part of the reading passage and determine whether it is used as a noun or as a verb. Then look up the word in a dictionary. What is the verb from which this word comes?

Similarly, the French word *face* may be either used as a noun or as an adverb. Locate the word in the part of the reading that describes the map. Determine whether it is used as a noun or as an adverb of location. Look up the word in the dictionary. Are there other uses?

Services la Samaritaine

La Samaritaine department store is proud of its history, culture, architecture, and tradition. Before reading the paragraphs, think about these four areas. What might the owners of the store want to promote?

Now read the passage and do the activities that follow.

Histoire

Construite par étape, de 1870 à 1927 sur le site même de la petite ville de Lutèce, la Samaritaine domine le plus vieux pont de Paris: le Pont-Neuf, l'Île de la Cité et tous ses monuments historiques. Aux alentours, vous revivrez la longue histoire de la ville des lumières. Plus d'un siècle après sa création par Ernest Cognacq, la Samaritaine est devenue un symbole du commerce qui rayonne à travers toute la capitale.

Culture

La Samaritaine, située à deux pas des deux centres culturels les plus importants de Paris (Musée du Louvre et Centre Georges Pompidou) et de l'une des plus belles cathédrales gothiques du monde, vit en bonne entente avec l'Art et l'Histoire. De l'autre côté de la Seine, le Quartier Latin avec la Sorbonne reste le berceau de la civilisation française.

Art nouveau

La Samaritaine est fière de ses magasins. En particulier du magasin 2 construit en pleine période de l'Art Nouveau (1906/1907 - 1926/1928) par le célèbre architecte belge Frantz Jourdain.

La façade dominant la Seine est un bel exemple de ce style très en vogue aujourd'hui; à l'intérieur, vous admirerez les superbes escaliers, les fresques et la verrière, qui témoignent de la plus belle facture de l'époque.

Tradition

La Samaritaine doit son nom à une ancienne pompe hydraulique (1603-1813) construite sur pilotis, jouxtant le Pont-Neuf et portant une décoration de plomb doré représentant Jésus et la Samaritaine (Évangile selon Saint-Jean). Cette pompe s'appelant la Samaritaine, symbole de l'accueil, le magasin a toujours attaché une attention particulière à l'excellent accueil de ses clients.

ACTIVITÉ 2

1. Read the four paragraphs from *la Samaritaine* brochure, then choose the best summary.
   a. *La Samaritaine* department store is an old and established enterprise.
   b. The stores are conveniently located in the heart of Paris.
   c. The stores were named after a hydraulic pump.
   d. All of the stores have been built recently.

2. Look at the *Histoire* paragraph more closely and answer the following questions.
   a. Near what famous bridge are the stores located?
   b. When was *la Samaritaine* founded? By whom?
   c. *La Samaritaine* was built on the site of what ancient city?

3. Look at the *Culture* paragraph more closely and answer the following questions.
   a. What two important cultural centers are near *la Samaritaine*?
   b. What famous cathedral is not far away?
   c. What university is located on the other side of the river?

4. Look at the *Art nouveau* paragraph more closely and answer the following questions.
   a. Which store has especially beautiful architecture?
   b. What style of architecture does this store represent?
   c. Inside the store, what features are striking?

5. Look at the *Tradition* paragraph more closely and answer the following questions.
   a. What was the store named after?
   b. Why is the name *la Samaritaine* particularly appropriate?
   c. In what way does the name reflect the store's principles?

BONUS: The paragraph on history mentions the *Pont Neuf*, while the paragraph on culture mentions the *Quartier Latin* and the *Sorbonne*. What can you find out about these places?

Dictionary Skills

One of the biggest challenges in using a dictionary is to know which word to look under. The problem arises because the dictionary does not list all words, but only certain forms of each word. For instance, most verbs are listed in the infinitive form. When you encounter a conjugated verb form such as *admirerez*, you first have to determine the infinitive of the verb. If you looked up *admirerez*, you would not find a listing. You have to derive the infinitive *admirer* to find out the meaning of the word.

Which verb does the word *vit* come from? Given the word alone, it may be difficult to guess. Look for it in context in the *Culture* paragraph. Does the context give you any clues?

Adjectives are also generally listed under only one form in a dictionary. Before looking up the adjective, you must transform the adjective to the masculine singular form. You must transform the word *ancienne* to *ancien* before looking it up.

In the phrase *un vieil établissement*, what word would you look up to find the meaning of the adjective *vieil*?

NOTES CULTURELLES

There are a number of famous, established department stores in Paris. These stores are collectively called *les grands magasins.* Their names are *le Printemps, les Galeries Lafayette,* and *la Samaritaine.*

In addition, there are also catalog-order establishments. *La Redoute* and *les Trois Suisses* are two famous ones.

PROJETS

1. *La Samaritaine* department store prides itself on its location, tradition, architecture, and sense of history. What other qualities might a department store want to promote? Using the INTERMARCHÉ advertisement in Chapter 17 as a model, write a short promotional piece for a department store of your choice.
2. Compare the promotional pieces for a local department store with that of *la Samaritaine.* Are there any differences? any similarities?

À L'ORAL

What qualities should be found in a good department store? Prepare a list of related questions in French, and poll your classmates. The following questions may be useful as a starting point.

—Est-ce qu'un bon magasin doit avoir une ancienne tradition?
—Est-ce que l'architecture du magasin est importante?
—Est-ce que la qualité de la marchandise est importante?
—Quels services voulez-vous dans un bon magasin?

GLOSSARY

A

à at, to
à côté de near
à peine scarcely
à pied on foot
d'abord first
s'absenter to be absent
l' **académie** *f.* academy
acadien *adj.* Acadian, Cajun
accessible *adj.* accessible
l' **accident** *m.* accident
accompagner to accompany
l' **accueil** *m.* greeting, welcome
accumuler to accumulate
l' **achat** *m.* purchase
acheter to buy
l' **acide** *m.* acid
l' **acteur** *m.* **(trice)** *f.* actor, actress
actuellement now, actually
l' **administration** *f.* administration
l' **admirateur** *m.* **(trice)** *f.* admirer
admirer to admire
l' **adolescent** *m.* adolescent
adopter to adopt
adorer to adore
l' **adresse** *f.* address
affecter to affect
l' **affection** *f.* affection
africain(ne) *adj.* African
l' **Afrique** Africa
l' **âge** *m.* age
l' **agence** *f.* agency
agir to act
agiter to agitate, to stir
l' **agneau** *m.* lamb
agréable *adj.* pleasant, nice
aigre *adj.* bitter
ailleurs elsewhere
aimer to love, to like

ainsi so, thus
l' **air** *m.* air
ajouter to add
l' **album** *m.* album
les **alentours** *m. pl.* neighborhood, surroundings
l' **Algérie** *f.* Algeria
alimentaire *adj.* alimentary, pertaining to food
l' **alimentation** *f.* food
l' **allée** *f.* alley
l' **Allemagne** *f.* Germany
allemand *adj.* German
aller to go
allô! hello (greeting on the phone)
allumer to light
alors then
alourdir to weigh down
les **Alpes** Alps (mountain range)
alphanumérique *adj.* alphanumeric
alsacien *adj.* Alsatian
l' **aluminium** *m.* aluminum
amener to bring along
américain *adj.* American
l' **Amérique** *f.* America
l' **ami** *m.* friend
amical *adj.* friendly
l' **amidon** *m.* starch
l' **amitié** *f.* friendship
l' **amour** *m.* love
amoureux *adj.* in love
amusant *adj.* amusing
l' **amusement** *m.* amusement
amuser to amuse
l' **an** *m.* year
analyser to analyze
l' **ananas** *m.* pineapple
l' **anchois** *m.* anchovy
ancien *adj.* old, ancient
anglais *adj.* English
l' **Angleterre** *f.* England
l' **animal** *m.* animal
l' **animation** *f.* activity, animation

l' **année** *f.* year
l' **anthème** *m.* anthem
l' **antiquité** *f.* antiquity
août August
apparaître to appear
l' **apparence** *f.* appearance
l' **apparition** *f.* apparition, ghost
appeler to call
apprécier to appreciate
apprivoiser to tame
appuyer to push
après after
l' **arbre** *m.* tree
l' **arc** *m.* arc
l' **architecte** *m.* architect
l' **argent** *m.* money, silver
l' **arôme** *m.* aroma, flavor
l' **arrêt** *m.* stop, bus stop, metro stop
arrière behind
arriver to arrive
l' **arrondissement** *m.* precinct in Paris
l' **art** *m.* art
l' **artichaut** *m.* artichoke
l' **article** *m.* article
l' **artifice** *m.* artifice
artificiel *adj.* artificial
l' **as** *m.* ace
l' **Asie** *f.* Asia
l' **aspiration** *f.* aspiration, inhaling
l' **assaisonnement** *m.* seasoning
assez enough
l' **assiette** *f.* plate
assimiler to assimilate
assorti *adj.* assorted
l' **assortiment** *m.* assortment
l' **assurance** *f.* insurance
l' **atelier** *m.* workshop
attacher to attach
attendre to wait
l' **attention** *f.* attention
l' **attraction** *f.* attraction
au at the, to the

aucun no one
l' **audace** *f.* daring
l' **auditorium** *m.* auditorium
aujourd'hui today
auquel to which
aussi also
autant as much
authentique *adj.* authentic
l' **auto** *f.* car
l' **autobus** *m.* bus
l' **auto-école** *f.* driving school
l' **automate** *m.* robot
automatique *adj.* automatic
automatiquement automatically
l' **automobiliste** *m.* driver
l' **autoroute** *f.* highway
autour around
autre other
avant before
avec with
l' **aventure** *f.* adventure
l' **avenue** *f.* avenue
l' **avion** *m.* airplane
l' **avocat** *m.* lawyer, avocado
avoir to have
avril April

B

la **baguette** French bread
le **bakchich** tip, gratuity
le **bal** ball, dance
la **balade** walk
balader to walk, to take a walk, to stroll
le **baladeur** Walkman
balancer to balance
le **balayeur** sweeper
le **ballet** ballet
le **ballon** ball, soccer ball
la **banane** banana
bancaire *adj.* pertaining to banks
la **banlieue** suburbs
la **banque** bank
bas *adj.* low
le **bas** stocking, nylon
la **base** base
basque *adj.* Basque, from the Basque region
la **bataille** battle

le **bateau** boat, ship
bâtir to build
beau (belle, bel) *adj.* beautiful, pretty
beaucoup much
la **beauté** beauty
belge *adj.* Belgian
la **belle** beauty
bénéficier to benefit from
le **Bénin** Benin (African country)
le **berceau** cradle
le **besoin** need
le **beurre** butter
beurrer to butter
la **bibliothèque** library
bien well
la **bière** beer
le **bifteck** beefsteak
la **bijouterie** jewelry, jeweller's shop
le **biniou** bagpipe
blanc (blanche) *adj.* white
bleu *adj.* blue
le **bleuet** bluet (flower)
le **bœuf** beef, cattle
la **boisson** drink
la **boîte** can, box, nightclub
bon *adj.* good
bonjour hello (greeting)
la **bonne** maid
le **bonnet** bonnet
le **bord** edge, border
la **bouche** mouth
la **boucherie** butcher shop
la **boulangerie** bakery
le **boulevard** boulevard
le **bout** end, piece
la **boutique** store, shop
brave *adj.* brave
la **Bretagne** Brittany
breton *adj.* Breton (from Brittany)
le **brie** Brie (cheese)
la **brioche** brioche (type of bread or pastry)
la **briocherie** brioche shop
britannique *adj.* from Great Britain
la **brocante** antique store, secondhand store
le **bronze** bronze
le **bruit** noise
le **brunch** brunch

brut *adj.* raw, rough
le **bureau** desk
le **bureau de poste** post office
le **Burkina Faso** Burkina Faso (African country)
le **bus** bus

C

ça this, that
le **cadeau** gift
le **cadre** frame
le **café** coffeehouse, coffee
le **café au lait** coffee with milk
le **café express** espresso coffee
la **cafétéria** cafeteria
le **cahier** notebook
la **caisse** cashier
la **caissette** small box
la **calculatrice** calculator
la **calorie** calorie
le **camembert** Camembert (cheese)
le **Cameroun** Cameroon (African country)
camerounais *adj.* from Cameroon
le **canard** duck
la **canette** duckling
le **canotage** canoeing
le **cantal** Cantal (cheese)
la **capitale** capital
les **câpres** capers
car because
le **carnaval** carnival
la **carotte** carrot
le **carrefour** intersection
la **carrière** career
la **carte** card, menu
le **cas** case
le **casque** helmet
la **casserole** pot, casserole
le **cassoulet** bean dish
le **catalogue** catalog
la **catégorie** category
la **cathédrale** cathedral
ce (cet, cette, ces) this, that, these, those
cela that
célèbre *adj.* famous
célébrer to celebrate
le **céleri** celery
celtique *adj.* Celtic, Irish
celui the one

cent one hundred
le **centime** cent
centrafricain *adj.* Central African
la **centrale** power station
le **centre** center
centré *adj.* centered
la **cérémonie** ceremony
certain *adj.* certain
certainement certainly
cesser to cease
c'est-à-dire that is to say
la **chaîne** chain
la **chambre** room
le **champignon** mushroom
les **Champs-Élysées** Champs-Élysées, avenue in Paris
changer to change
la **chanson** song
chanter to sing
le **chanteur** singer
la **chapelle** chapel
chaque each, every
la **charcuterie** delicatessen
charger to charge, to load
le **chasseur** hunter
chaud *adj.* hot
le **chausson** turnover
le **cheddar** cheddar cheese
le **chef** chief, head
le **chef de pupitre** orchestra conductor
le **chef-d'œuvre** masterpiece
le **chemin** road, way, path
le **chèque** check
cher *adj.* dear, expensive
chercher to look for
chez at the home of, at the place of
le **chien** dog
le **chiffre** number
chinois *adj.* Chinese
le **chocolat** chocolate
le **chœur** choir
choisir to choose
le **choix** choice
la **chose** thing
le **chou** cabbage
le **chou-fleur** cauliflower
le **cidre** cider
le **ciel (cieux)** sky

le **cimetière** cemetery
le **cinéma** movie theater
cinq five
la **circonstance** circumstance
le **circuit** circuit
le **cirque** circus
la **citrate** citrate (chemical)
citrique *adj.* citric
le **citron** lemon
la **civilisation** civilization
clairement clearly
le **client** customer
le **climat** climate, weather
le **cm (centimètre)** centimeter
le **Coca(-Cola)** Coca-Cola
le **cocktail** cocktail
le **code** code
le **cœur** heart
le **coiffeur** hairdresser
le **coin** corner
le **colis** package
la **collection** collection
le **côlon** colon, large intestine
colonial *adj.* colonial
la **colonie** colony
la **colonisation** colonization
le **colorant** coloring agent
combien how much
le **comble** the utmost
la **comédie** comedy
la **commande** order
commander to order
comme like, as
commencer to begin
comment how
le **commentaire** commentary
le **commerce** commerce
commercial *adj.* commercial
commun *adj.* common
la **communication** communication
communiquer to communicate
les **Comores** Comoro Islands
compact *adj.* compact, small
la **compagnie** company
complet *adj.* complete
complètement completely

compliquer to complicate
le **comportement** behavior
se comporter to behave
composé *adj.* composed, complex
composer to dial a telephone, to compose
comprendre to understand
compris *adj.* understood
le **compte** account, sum
compter to count
concernant concerning, about
le **concert** concert
le **concombre** cucumber
le **concours** contest
le **conducteur** driver
conduire to drive
se conduire to behave
la **conduite** behavior
le **confetti** confetti
la **confiance** faith
confirmer to confirm
le **conflit** conflict
confortable *adj.* comfortable
le **Congo** Congo
la **connaissance** knowledge
connaître to know
connu *adj.* known
le **conseil** advice
par conséquent consequently, as a result
conserver to conserve, to preserve
considérer to consider
le **consommateur** consumer
la **construction** construction
construit *adj.* built
content *adj.* happy
contingent *adj.* contingent
continuer to continue
contrairement on the other hand
contrôler to control
convenir to suit
copieux *adj.* plentiful
la **corde** rope
la **cordonnerie** shoe repair shop
le **costume** suit
la **côte** coast

la **couleur** color
le **couloir** hall, corridor
le **coup** hit, blow
la **coupe** cup, trophy
couper to cut
courageux *adj.* courageous
la **course** race
la **courtoisie** courtesy
coûter to cost
le **couvert** place setting
couvrir to cover
le **créateur** creator
la **création** creation
créer to create
la **crevette** shrimp
crier to yell, to cry
croire to believe
le **croissant** crescent roll
le **crooner** crooner, singer
le **croque-monsieur** ham and cheese sandwich
cru *adj.* raw
les **crudités** *f.* raw vegetables
le **cube** cube
la **cuillère** spoon
la **cuisine** kitchen
cuisiné *adj.* cooked
culturel *adj.* cultural
le **cyclisme** bicycle racing
le **cyclomoteur** moped

D

le **danger** danger
dangereux *adj.* dangerous
dans in, within
la **danse** dance
danser to dance
la **date** date
de of, from
débrancher to disconnect
décembre December
décider to decide
déclarer to declare
la **décoration** decoration
découper to cut out
la **découverte** discovery
découvrir to discover
décrocher to pick up the phone
le **défilé** parade
déjà already
déjeuner to lunch

le **délai** delay
délicieux *adj.* delicious
la **demande** request
demander to ask
le **démarreur** starter
demi half
la **demi-journée** half-day
la **dent** tooth
le **départ** start
le **département** department
dépasser to pass, to surpass
déplacer to move, to displace
déporter to deport
déposer to deposit
depuis since
le **dernier** last
le **déroulement** unfolding
derrière behind
le **descendant** descendant
le **désert** desert
désiré *adj.* wanted
désirer to want, to desire
le **dessert** dessert
le **dessin** drawing, sketch
détailler to itemize, specify
la **détaxe** tax refund, rebate
détester to hate
deux two
le **développement** development
devenir to become
devoir to have to
le **devoir** homework
le **diabolo** a float, a carbonated ice cream drink
le **dialecte** dialect
la **différence** difference
différent *adj.* different
le **dimanche** Sunday
la **dinde** turkey
la **diplomatie** diplomacy
dire to say
directement directly
la **direction** direction
la **discipline** discipline
la **discothèque** disco
disponible *adj.* available
disposer to dispose
la **distinction** distinction
la **distribution** distribution
divers *adj.* diverse, sundry

le **divertissement** amusement
diviser to divide
le **documentaire** documentary
le **dollar** dollar
le **domicile** home
dominer to dominate
donc then, therefore
donner to give
dont whose
doré *adj.* golden, gilded
double double
douillet *adj.* cosy
le **doute** doubt
doux (douce) *adj.* sweet
dresser to train; to hold up
la **droguerie** pharmacy
le **droit** right, law
drôle *adj.* funny
dur *adj.* hard

E

l' **eau** *f.* water
l' **ébullition** *f.* boiling
l' **éclair** *m.* eclair pastry, lightning bolt
éclater to burst, to explode
l' **école** *f.* school
économique *adj.* economical
l' **écrivain** *m.* writer
l' **édition** *f.* edition
effectuer to effectuate, to do
l' **effort** *m.* effort
également equally
l' **église** *f.* church
égyptien *adj.* Egyptian
l' **électricité** *f.* electricity
électrique *adj.* electric
l' **électro-ménager** *m.* home appliances
élu *adj.* elected
embrasser to kiss, to hug
l' **empereur** *m.* emperor
l' **empire** *m.* empire
l' **emploi** *m.* use
l' **employé** *m.* employee
employer to use
emporter to carry away
emprunter to borrow
en in
encore more, still

l' **énergie** *f.* energy
l' **enfant** *f.* child
engager to engage
l' **enquête** *f.* investigation
enregistrer to record, to enroll
l' **enseigne** *f.* sign
ensemble together
ensuite then, following
l' **entente** *f.* agreement
entier *adj.* whole
entraîner to train
entre between
l' **entrer** to enter, to come in
l' **entretien** *m.* maintenance, meeting
l' **envie** *f.* envy, want
environ about, around
envoyer to send
l' **épaisseur** *f.* thickness
l' **épaule** *f.* shoulder
l' **épice** *f.* spice
épicé *adj.* spicy
l' **épicerie** *f.* grocery store
l' **épisode** *m.* episode
l' **époque** *f.* time, era
l' **épouvante** *f.* horror
équestre *adj.* equestrian
équilibré *adj.* balanced
équipé *adj.* equipped
l' **équipement** *m.* equipment
l' **érable** *m.* maple tree
érailler to fray, to make (voice) hoarse
l' **escalier** *m.* staircase
l' **escalope** *f.* thin cut of meat
l' **escargot** *m.* snail
l' **espace** *m.* space
l' **Espagne** *f.* Spain
espagnol *adj.* Spanish
l' **espion** *m.* spy
essayer to try
l' **essence** *f.* extract
essentiel *adj.* essential, important
l' **est** *m.* east
établir to establish
l' **établissement** *m.* establishment
l' **étape** *f.* leg, step
l' **état** *m.* state
etc. and so on
étendre to spread
ethnique *adj.* ethnic

l' **étoile** *f.* star
étonnant *adj.* astonishing
étourdi *adj* dizzy, thoughtless
être to be
étrusque *adj.* Etruscan
l' **euromarché** *m.* European market
l' **Europe** *f.* Europe
l' **évaluation** *f.* evaluation
l' **évangile** *m.* gospel
éveiller to wake up
évidemment evidently
exactement exactly
excéder to exceed
excellent *adj.* excellent
l' **excursion** *f.* excursion
l' **exemple** *m.* example
exister to exist
l' **exploration** *f.* exploration
l' **exposition** *f.* exposition
l' **express** *m.* espresso coffee
exprimer to express

F

la **fabrication** manufacture
la **façade** facade of building
la **face** face
en face de facing
facile *adj.* easy
facilement easily
faciliter to facilitate
la **facture** bill
faire to do
falloir to have to
familial *adj.* familial (of the family)
la **famille** family
fanatique *adj.* fanatical
le **fast-food** fast food
il faut one must
faux *adj.* wrong, false
la **fécule** starch
la **femme** woman, wife
fermer to close
le **festival** festival
la **fête** holiday, feast
le **feu** fire
les **feux d'artifice** fireworks
la **feuille** sheet, leaf
février February
fiable *adj.* reliable
la **fiction** fiction

fidèle *adj.* faithful, true
la **fidélité** faithfulness
fier *adj.* proud
le **fil** thread
le **filet** net, shopping net
la **fille** girl, daughter
le **film** film, movie
la **fin** end
final *adj.* final
flamand *adj.* Flemish
la **fleur** flower
le **fleuve** river
le **flic** policeman, cop (familiar)
le **flipper** pinball machine
fluo(rescent) *adj.* fluorescent, glows in the dark
le **foie** liver
la **foire** fair
la **fois** time
folklorique *adj.* folkloric
foncer to forge ahead, speed ahead
fonctionner to function, to work
le **fond** end, bottom
fondre to melt
la **formation** formation
former to form
formidable *adj.* great, terrific
la **formule** formula
le **fossé** ditch, moat
fou (folle) *adj.* crazy, mad
le **four** oven
la **fourrure** fur
le **foyer** home, household
la **fraîcheur** coolness, freshness
frais *adj.* fresh
la **fraise** strawberry
le **franc** franc (French money)
français *adj.* French
franchement frankly
francophone *adj.* French speaking
le **franglais** French-English
frapper to hit
fréquemment frequently
fréquent *adj.* frequent
le **frère** brother
la **fresque** fresco painting
le **frisson** shiver

froid *adj.* cold
la **froidure** coldness
le **fromage** cheese
la **frontière** border, frontier
le **fruit** fruit
fumé *adj.* smoked
le **futur** future

G

le **Gabon** Gabon (African country)
la **gamme** range, assortment
garantir to guarantee
le **garçon** boy, son
garder to keep
la **gare** train station
la **garniture** garnish
le **gâteau** cake
gauche *adj.* left; inelegant
le **gendarme** policeman
général *adj.* general
généralement generally
la **génération** generation
les **gens** people
le **geste** gesture
la **glace** ice cream
glacé *adj.* cold, icy
le **glutamate monosodique** monosodium glutamate (chemical)
gothique *adj.* gothic
le **gouverneur** governor
grâce à thanks to
la **graisse** fat
grand *adj.* big, large
graphique *adj.* graphic
gras *adj.* fatty, greasy
gratuit *adj.* free
gratuitement freely
la **gravure** engraving
la **Grèce** Greece
grec(que) *adj.* Greek
la **grenouille** frog
la **grève** strike
la **grille** grill
le **groupe** group
le **gruyère** Gruyere cheese
la **guerre** war
le **guide** guide
guider to guide
la **Guinée** Guinea (African country)
la **guitare** guitar
la **Guyane** Guyana
le **gymnase** gymnasium

H

l' **habitant** *m.* inhabitant
habiter to live
le **hall** hallway, corridor
les **halles** *f.* food market
le **haricot** bean
l' **herbe** *f.* herb
le **héro** hero
hésiter to hesitate
l' **heure** *f.* hour
heureusement happily
heureux *adj.* happy
hier yesterday
l' **histoire** *f.* history
historique *adj.* historical
l' **hiver** *m.* winter
le **hockey** hockey
hollandais *adj.* Dutch; hollandaise (sauce)
l' **homme** *m.* man
l' **honneur** *m.* honor
l' **horaire** *m.* hours, schedule
l' **horizon** *m.* horizon
l' **horreur** *f.* horror
l' **hôtel** *m.* hotel, public building
l' **huile** *f.* oil
humain *adj.* human
l' **humidité** *f.* humidity
hydraulique *adj.* hydraulic
hydrogéné *adj.* hydrogenated
l' **hygiène** *f.* hygiene
hygiénique *adj.* hygienic
l' **hypermarché** *m.* large supermarket

I

l' **iceberg** *m.* iceberg
ici here
idéal *adj.* ideal
l' **idée** *f.* idea
l' **identité** *f.* identity
l' **île** *f.* island
imiter to imitate
immédiat *adj.* immediate
immédiatement immediately
important *adj.* important
inaugurer to inaugurate
inclus *adj.* included
l' **inconnu** *m.* unknown
l' **inconscient** *m.* subconscious, unconscious

indéniable *adj.* undeniable
l' **indépendance** *f.* independence
indépendant *adj.* independent
indiquer to indicate, to show
indiscutable *adj.* indisputable
l' **infante** *f.* princess
inférieur *adj.* inferior
influer to influence
l' **information** *f.* information
informer to inform
l' **infraction** *f.* infraction, breaking of the law
l' **ingrédient** *m.* ingredient
instantané *adj.* instantaneous
intégré *adj.* integrated
intéressant *adj.* interesting
intéresser to interest
l' **intérêt** *m.* interest
intérieur *adj.* interior
international *adj.* international
interpréter to interpret
interroger to interrogate
irlandais *adj.* Irish
l' **Irlande** *f.* Ireland
l' **Italie** *f.* Italy
italien *adj.* Italian
l' **ivoire** *f.* ivory

J

jamais never
le **jambon** ham
janvier January
japonais *adj.* Japanese
le **jardin** garden
le **jardinier** gardener
jaune yellow
jeudi Thursday
jeune *adj.* young
jouer to play
le **jouet** toy
le **jour** day; **du jour** special of the day
jouxtant next to
juillet July
juin June
le **juke-boxe** juke box

jurer to swear
le **jus** juice
jusqu'à until, up to

K

le **kaiser** Kaiser, king
le **kilomètre** kilometer
km *abrev.* kilometer
km/h *abrev.* **kilomètre heure** kilometer per hour

L

là there
laisser to leave, to let
le **lait** milk
la **laitue** lettuce
la **lamelle** strip
la **langue** tongue
latin *adj.* Latin
léger *adj.* light
le **légume** vegetable
la **lettre** letter
leur their
la **liberté** liberty
le, la **libraire** bookseller
libre *adj.* free
le **lieu** place
la **ligne** line
la **limitation** limit
limité *adj.* limited
la **limonade** lemonade
la **liste** list
le **lit** bed
le **litre** liter
la **livraison** delivery
livrer to deliver
localisé *adj.* localized
la **location** rental
la **loi** law
le **loisir** free time, leisure
la **longueur** length
lorsque then
le **Louvre** Louvre (museum in Paris)
la **lumière** light
lundi Monday
la **lune** moon
Lutèce *f.* former name of Paris
le **lycée** high school

M

le **macaroni** macaroni
la **machine** machine

le **magasin** store
mai May
la **main** hand
la **mairie** city hall
mais but
le **maïs** corn
la **maison** house
malheureusement unfortunately
le **Mali** Mali (African country)
la **maman** mom, mother
le **manège** merry-go-round
manger to eat
maniable *adj.* manageable
la **manière** manner
manquer to miss, to lack
la **mantille** head scarf (Spain)
le **maquillage** makeup
le **marbre** marble
le **marchand** merchant
la **marchandise** merchandise
marcher to walk, to work
mardi Tuesday
la **marge** margin
le **mari** husband
marier to marry, to wed
le **marin** sailor
la **marine** navy
le **Maroc** Morocco (North African country)
mars March
la **Martinique** Martinique (Caribbean country)
le **match de foot** soccer game
le **matelot** sailor
le **matériel** hardware
la **maternelle** kindergarten
la **Mauritanie** Mauritania (African country)
mauvais *adj.* bad, evil
le **maximum** maximum
la **mayonnaise** mayonnaise
médiéval *adj.* medieval
médiocre *adj.* mediocre
le **mégacentre** large store
mélanger to mix
la **mélodie** melody
le **membre** member
même even
la **mémoire** memory
la **menthe** mint

mentir to lie
le **menu** menu
la **mer** sea
merci thank you
mercredi Wednesday
la **mère** mother
la **météo** weather report
le **métier** job, position
le **métro** subway
midi noon
la **mie** bread dough
mieux better
mijoter to simmer
mille *m.* one thousand
million *m.* a million
le **minéral** mineral
la **miniature** miniature
le **Minitel** Minitel (information appliance)
minuit midnight
la **minute** minute
mi-temps half-time
mi-voix spoken softly
Mme *abrev.* Madam, Mrs.
le **mobilier** furniture
la **mobylette** moped
la **mode** fashion
le **modèle** model
moderne *adj.* modern
moi me, I
moins less, least
le **mois** month
la **moitié** half
le **moment** moment
mon my
le **monde** world
mondial *adj.* global
mondialement globally
monsieur Mr., Sir
la **montagne** mountain
monter to climb
la **montre** watch
montrer to show
le **monument** monument
le **mot** word
le **moteur** motor, engine
la **moto** motorcycle
la **motocyclette** motorcycle
le **mousquetaire** musketeer
la **moutarde** mustard
moyen *adj.* average
le **mur** wall
le **musée** museum
musical *adj.* musical
la **musique** music

N

n'importe no matter
naître to be born
natal *adj.* native
national *adj.* national
nature *adj* plain
le **navet** turnip
naviguer to navigate
nécessaire *adj.* necessary
la **nécessité** necessity
négliger to neglect
la **neige** snow
nerveux *adj.* nervous
nettoyer to clean
le **nettoyeur** cleaner
le **nez** nose
nier to deny, to negate
le **Niger** Niger (African country)
le **niveau** level
nocturne *adj.* nocturnal
noir *adj.* black
la **noix** nut, walnut
le **nom** name
le **nombre** number
nombreux *adj.* numerous
nommer to name
non no
le **nord** north
normal *adj.* normal
notre our
la **nourriture** food
nouveau *adj.* new
novembre November
la **nuit** night
le **numéro** number
nutritif *adj.* nutritional

O

l' **Oasis** *m.* sparkling water
l' **objet** *m.* object
obligatoire *adj.* required
l' **observatoire** *m.* observatory
l' **occasion** *f.* occasion, opportunity
occidental *adj.* occidental, Western
occuper to occupy
l' **Océanie** *f.* Oceania
octobre October
l' **odeur** *f.* odor
l' **œuf** *m.* egg
offert *adj.* offered
l' **office** *m.* office

officiel *adj.* official
l' **offre** *f.* offer
offrir to offer
l' **oie** *f.* goose
l' **oignon** *m.* onion
l' **oiseau** *m.* bird
l' **okra** *f.* okra
l' **olive** *f.* olive
l' **omelette** *f.* omelet
on one, someone
l' **oncle** *m.* uncle
oral *adj.* oral
l' **orange** *f.* orange
l' **Orangina** *m.* Orangina (orange drink)
orchestral *adj.* orchestral
l' **orchestre** *m.* orchestra
l' **ordure** *f.* garbage
l' **orge** *f.* barley
oriental *adj.* oriental
l' **orientation** *f.* orientation
orienter to orient
l' **origan** *m.* oregano
originaire *adj.* originally from
l' **origine** *f.* origin
ou or
où where
oublier to forget
l' **ouest** *m.* west
oui yes
ouvert *adj.* open
l' **ouverture** *f.* overture, opening
ouvrir to open

P

les **P.T.T.** French postal administration
la **pacane** pecan (Canadian)
le **paiement** payment
le **pain** bread
le **pamplemousse** grapefruit
le **panneau** panel
le **papa** dad, father
par by
le **parc** parc
parce que because
parcourir to scan
le **parent** parent, relative
parfait *adj.* perfect
parfois sometimes
parisien *adj.* Parisian
le **parking** parking lot

parler to speak
parmi among
particulier *adj.* particular
la **partie** party, part
partir to leave
partout everywhere
le **pas** footstep
passer to pass
la **patate** potato
le **pâté** kind of spread, usually with liver
la **pâtisserie** bakery
la **patrie** fatherland
payer to pay
le **pays** country
la **peau** skin
la **pêche** fishing
la **peinture** painting
pendant during, while
penser to think
le **penseur** thinker
la **perception** perception
perdre to lose
le **père** father
la **période** period
la **périphérie** periphery, outside
permanent *adj.* permanent
permettre to allow, to permit
le **permis** license
le **permis de conduire** driver's license
le **persil** parsley
le **personnage** charactor in a play or novel
personne nobody, no one
petit *adj.* small
peu little, few
le **peuple** people
la **pharmacie** drug store, pharmacy
la **photo** picture, photo
la **photographie** photograph, photo
le/la **pianiste** pianist
la **pièce** piece, play
le **pied** foot
le **piéton** pedestrian
le **pignon** gable
le **pilote** pilot
le **pilotis** piling
la **pintade** pheasant-like bird

la **pinte** pint
piquant *adj.* spicy, hot
le **pique-nique** picnic
la **piscine** swimming pool
la **place** place
la **plaine** plain
le **plaisir** pleasure
le **plan** plan, map
plat *adj.* flat
le **plat** dish
plein *adj.* full
le **plomb** lead
plonger to dive
la **pluie** rain
plupart most
plus more
plusieurs many
la **poche** pocket
le **poêlon** small skillet
le **poème** poem
le **poète** poet
le **point** period, point
la **pointe** point, cape (sea)
la **poire** pear
le **pois** pea
le **poivron** bell pepper
le **policier** police officer
la **politique** politics
la **pomme** apple
la **pompe** pump
le **pompier** fireman
le **pont** bridge, long week-
end
populaire *adj.* popular
la **population** population
le **porc** pig, pork
le **port** port
la **porte** door
la **portée** reach, range
porter to wear
poser to set down
posséder to own
la **possibilité** possibility
possible *adj.* possible
postal *adj.* postal
la **poste** post office
le **poste** job, employment
le **potage** soup
le **pouding** pudding
la **poudrerie** gunpowder
factory, flurry of snow
le **poulet** chicken
pour for
pourquoi why
pouvoir to be able to
pratique *adj.* practical

pratiquer to practice
préférer to prefer
premier *adj.* first
prendre to take
préparer to prepare
près de near
la **présence** presence
présenter to introduce, to
present
le **président** president
pressé *adj.* pressed
la **pression** pressure
prêt *adj.* ready
prêt-à-porter ready-to-
wear
la **preuve** proof
principal *adj.* principal,
main
le **printemps** spring
le **prix** price
probablement probably
le **problème** problem
le **procès** lawsuit
le **procès-verbal** ticket
la **proclamation** proclamation
produire to produce
le **produit** product
le **professeur** professor,
teacher
professionnel *adj.* pro-
fessional
profiter to profit
programmable *adj.* programmable
le **programme** program
programmer to program
le **projet** project
la **prolongation** lengthen-
ing, prolongation
la **promenade** walk
proposer to propose
la **propreté** cleanliness
la **protection** protection
la **protéine** protein
prouver to prove
la **province** province
la **proximité** proximity,
nearness
prudent *adj.* prudent,
wise
la **publicité** publicity
publier to publish
la **puissance** power
puissant *adj.* powerful
le **pupitre** desk

les **Pyrénées** Pyrenees
mountains

Q

le **quadricycle** four-wheeled
bicycle
le **quai** dock, platform
qualifier to qualify
la **qualité** quality
quand when
la **quantité** quantity
le **quart** quart, quarter
le **quartier** neighborhood
le **quartz** quartz
quasi almost, quasi
quatre four
**quel (quels, quelle,
quelles)** which
quelque *adj.* some
la **question** question
qui who, whom
la **quiche** quiche pie
quinze fifteen
quitter to quit, to leave
quoi what
quotidien *adj.* daily

R

la **race** race
la **radio** radio
le **radis** radish
la **rafale** burst
le **raisin** grape
la **raison** reason
râpé *adj.* grated
rapide *adj.* rapid, fast
la **rapidité** speed
le **rappel** recall, reminder
rarement rarely
rassurer to reassure
le **rat** rat
rater to miss
la **RATP** *abrev.* Parisian
Transport Company
rauque *adj.* hoarse
le **rayon** aisle
rayonner to radiate
la **réalisation** realization
la **réalité** reality
récent *adj.* recent
le **récepteur** receiver
recevoir to receive
la **recherche** research
récompenser to reward
recomposer to recompose

la **reconstitution** reconstitution

le **recueil** anthology, collection

la **Redoute** French mail order company

réduit *adj.* reduced

la **référence** reference

le **réflexe** reflex

le **refrain** refrain, chorus

refuser to refuse

regarder to look

la **région** region

la **règle** rule

regretter to regret

la **relation** relation

remercier to thank

remplacer to replace

remplir to fill up, to fill out

remuer to stir

le **rendez-vous** date, meeting

renforcer to reinforce

le **renseignement** information

renseigner to inform, to tell

réparer to repair

le **répondeur** telephone answering machine

répondre to answer

la **réponse** answer

repousser to push away

le **représentant** salesman, representative

la **république** republic

la **République Malgache** Malagasy Republic

le **réseau** network

la **réservation** reservation

réserver to make a reservation

le **réservoir** reservoir, tank

la **résidence** home

résister to resist

résoudre to solve

respecter to respect

responsable *adj.* responsible

ressembler to resemble, to look like

le **restaurant** restaurant

la **restauration** restoration

restauré restored

le **reste** rest, remainder

rester to stay

le **résultat** result

le **retour** return

retourner to return

réunir to gather, to reunite

réveiller to wake up

revenir to return

revivre to relive

riche *adj.* rich

rien nothing

le **risque** risk

la **robe** dress

le **robot** robot

le **rock-blues** rock-blues

le **rôle** role, part in a play

romain *adj.* Roman

rond *adj.* round

la **rondelle** round slice

le **roquefort** Roquefort cheese

le **rôti** roast

la **roue** wheel

rouge *adj.* red

la **route** road

routier *adj.* of roads

royal *adj.* royal

la **rue** street

S

la **saison** season

la **salade** salad

salé *adj.* salty

la **salle** room, hall

la **Samaritaine** Parisian department store

samedi Saturday

le **sandwich** sandwich

le **sang-froid** coolness, composure

sans without

satisfait *adj.* satisfied

la **sauce** sauce

le **saucisson** sausage

sauté *adj.* pan-fried

sauvage *adj.* wild

le **savant** scholar

la **saveur** taste

savoir to know

la **science** science

scientifique *adj.* scientific

le **scooter** scooter

le **sculpteur** sculptor

la **sculpture** sculpture

la **séance** showing

la **seconde** second

le **secret** secret

la **sécurité** security

la **séduction** seduction

la **séguedille** Spanish dance

la **Seine** Seine river

le **séjour** stay

le **sel** salt

selon according to

la **semaine** week

le **Sénégal** Senegal (African country)

sensationnel *adj.* sensational

septembre September

la **série** series

sérieux *adj.* serious

le **service** service

servir to serve

seul *adj.* alone

seulement only

le **shopping** shopping

si if, so

le **siècle** century

le **siège** seat

signer to sign

simple *adj.* simple

simplement simply

la **simplicité** simplicity

le **sirop** syrup

le **site** site

situé *adj.* situated, located

situer to locate, to situate

le **ski** ski

la **SNCF** *abrev.* French railroad company

le **sodium** sodium

la **sœur** sister

le **soir** evening

la **soirée** evening

le **soleil** sun

solitaire *adj.* alone

solo solo

la **solution** solution

le **soprano** soprano

le **sorbet** sherbet

la **sortie** exit

le **soufflé** soufflé (dish)

souhaiter to wish

le **souk** bazaar

la **soupe** soup

sous under

le **sous-sol** basement

souterrain *adj.* underground

souvent often
spécial *adj.* special
spécialement specially
spécialisé *adj.* specialized
le **spécialiste** specialist
la **spécialité** specialty
le **spectacle** spectacle
le **sport** sport
le **stade** stadium
la **station** station
stationner to park
la **statistique** statistic
le **style** style
le **succès** success
le **sucre** sugar
le **sud** south
suffir to be enough
la **suite** continuation, following
le **suivant** next one, following
suivre to follow
le **sujet** subject
super *adj.* super
superbe *adj.* superb
la **supérette** small grocery store
le **supermarché** supermarket
supplémentaire *adj.* supplementary, extra
supplémenter to supplement
sur on
sûr *adj.* sure
surtout above all
le **symbole** symbol
sympathique *adj.* likeable
le **système** system

T

la **table** table
la **table d'orientation** panoramic view
le **tableau** board
la **taille** size
taire to be quiet
le **talent** talent
le **tambour** drum
tandis que while
taper to hit
le **tapioca** tapioca
tard late

le **tarif** tariff, fare, price
la **tarte** tart
la **tartelette** small tart
le **taureau** bull
le **taxi** taxi
le **Tchad** Chad (African country)
le **téléfilm** TV film
le **téléphone** telephone
la **télévision** television
telle such
témoigner to testify, to witness
la **température** temperature
temporaire *adj.* temporary
le **temps** time, weather
de temps en temps from time to time
tenir to hold
la **terre** earth, ground
le **territoire** territory
la **tête** head
le **textile** textile, cloth
le **thé** tea
le **théâtre** theater
le **thon** tuna
la **tisane** herbal tea
le **titre** title, stock
le **titre restaurant** restaurant coupon
le **Togo** Togo (African country)
toi you (familiar)
la **tomate** tomato
ton your
la **tonne** ton
totaliser to sum up, to add up
le **toubib** doctor (familiar)
la **touche** key on a keyboard
toujours always
la **Tour Eiffel** Eiffel Tower
le **tourisme** tourism
le **tournage** filming
tourner to turn, to film
tous all, everyone
tout all, everything
tracer to trace
la **tradition** tradition
le **train** train
en train de in the process of
le **traité** treaty
la **tranche** slice, part
transformer to transform

la **transmission** transmission
le **transport** transportation
transporter to transport
le **travail** work
travailler to work
à travers crosswise, the wrong way
traverser to cross
la **trentaine** about 30
très very
le **tricycle** tricycle
le **trio** trio, three
triompher to triumph, to be victorious
trois three
troisième third
trop too much, too many
trouver to find
tuer to kill
se tuer to kill oneself
le **tuner** tuner
la **Tunisie** Tunisia (North African country)
le **tunnel** tunnel
le **type** type

U

ultime *adj.* last
uni *adj.* united
universel *adj.* universal
l' **université** *f.* university
utiliser to use

V

la **valeur** value
la **vanille** vanilla
varier to vary
la **variété** variety
le **veau** veal
vécu *p.p.* lived
végétal *adj.* vegetal, from vegetables
végétarien *adj.* vegetarian
le **véhicule** vehicle
le **vélo** bicycle
vendre to sell
vendredi Friday
venir to come
le **vent** wind
verbal *adj.* verbal
véritable *adj.* true
la **verrière** stained glass window
vers toward
vert *adj.* green

le **vêtement** clothes
le **vétérinaire** veterinary
vider to empty
la **vie** life
vieux (vieille) *adj.* old
la **villa** villa
le **village** village
la **ville** town
le **vin** wine
la **vinaigrette** vinegar sauce
vingt twenty
la **visite** visit
visiter to visit
le **visiteur** visitor
la **vitamine** vitamin
vite quickly
la **vitesse** speed
vivant *adj.* alive

vivre to live
la **vogue** fashion
voici here
voilà there
voir to see
le **voisin** neighbor
la **voiture** car
la **volaille** poultry
le **volant** steering wheel
volontiers willingly
vos your
le **vote** vote
votre your
vouloir to want to
le **voyage** travel
voyager to travel
le **voyageur** traveler
vrai *adj.* true

la **vue** view, vista

W

le **western** western (type of film)
le **wolof** Wolof (African language)

Y

y there

Z

le **Zaïre** Zaire (African country)